GYLES BRANDRETH'S
COMPLETE BOOK OF HOME ENTERTAINMENT

Books by Gyles Brandreth

Created in Captivity
Brandreth's Party Games
Brandreth's Bedroom Book
Games for Trains, Planes and Wet Days
Knight Book of Party Games
Knight Book of Christmas Fun
Aladdin
Cinderella
Mother Goose
Discovering Pantomime
I Scream for Ice Cream

Gyles Brandreth's
Complete Book of Home Entertainment

Shire Publications Ltd.

For
Jennifer, Virginia, Hester
and Ben

CONTENTS

INTRODUCTION

Fun is what this book is all about. Indeed, I would have called it my *Complete Book of Home Fun* but for the fact that 'fun' seems such a simple word for such a sophisticated age. The entertainments described in the pages that follow are designed to amuse and divert, not to inform and instruct. I haven't told you how to become a chess champion or win a fortune at bridge, let alone how to build a boat in a bottle, because the book isn't about complex pastimes, hobbies and home crafts. It's about a hundred and one entertaining ways to keep yourself and your family and friends amused and out of mischief for three hundred and sixty-five days in the year.

Rest assured — you don't need to have been to drama school to enjoy the Art of Recitation and being a member of the Magic Circle won't help you one bit when you come to the chapter of tricks. All this volume requires of you is a rough ability to read and a desire to have a good time.

Needless to say, I have had a *marvellous* time writing the book, because I have tried and tested all the games and tricks and ideas — except, of course, the novel but near-lethal entertainments described in Chapter 12. Naturally, I have been helped enormously by all sorts of people, not least by David Farris who provided the illustrations. In particular I must thank three ladies: Miss Annabel Olivier-Wright (for her generous research), Miss Selena Cadell (for her nimble fingers) and Miss Michele Brown (for her coffee and comfort).

Having warned you that I'm not in earnest and having thanked my invaluable helpers, it only remains for me to hope that you enjoy the book. However, if you don't, don't despair. You can always entertain your friends by picking up *Gyles Brandreth's Complete Book of Home*

Entertainment and tearing it in two at a stroke. They won't believe the feat possible — but it is, providing you know the secret (the sort of secret with which this volume is packed). Simply bake the book for an hour in a low oven. Remove it, cool it and then let rip.

1. PARLOUR GAMES

The British have had parlours for longer than most and the British have played parlour games for longer than any. These games are all classics of their kind and have stood the test of time. Their great merit is their flexibility. Most of them can be played with five, fifty or five times fifty players and all of them will add to the pleasure of an afternoon or evening of home entertainment.

Ad-lib

One player leaves the room, while all the others agree on a descriptive and not over-obscure adverb. It must be descriptive because when the outsider returns they must all behave and must answer questions in the manner of the adverb. It mustn't be too obscure because the outsider has got to try to guess it. Among adverbs that are fun to perform and not impossible to guess are:

brutally	harshly	pompously	softly
casually	hysterically	romantically	sweetly
cheekily	laughingly	rudely	terrifyingly
emotionally	mournfully	sadly	viciously
feebly	piously	slowly	

Apple Ducking

If you have a keen sense of humour — and a firm set of teeth — you can play this game all on your own. It's more fun, however, played with a crowd. You need a large tub of water to put in the centre of the room and a dozen apples (say, ten eating and two cooking) to put in the water. On the command 'Go' the players rush towards the tub, kneel down with their hands behind their backs and attempt to lift the bobbing apples out of the water with their teeth and mouths. Nobody wins, but the player who secures the most apples has to reveal the name and address of his dentist.

Authentic Hunt the Thimble

Along with steam engines and kippers on railway trains, thimbles are harder to find these days than once they were. However, if you do happen to be the proud owner of an authentic English thimble you must celebrate the fact by playing a round or two of this age-old parlour game.

Get all the players to leave the room and, while they're out of the way, place your thimble in some unlikely spot in the room. It can be anywhere, but it must be visible to all the players whatever their height and must be in a position where it can be seen without anyone having to move anything to see it. Once you've 'hidden' it, invite the players in and get them to hunt for it. As soon as a player spots it, he says nothing, but sits down quietly. The last player to spot the thimble is the loser and has the job of 'hiding' it for the next round.

Blind Man's Buff

Long before the age of the parlour this game was being played. Nobody knows if Adam and Eve enjoyed it in the Garden of Eden, but without a doubt it was a popular children's game by the time Moses was a boy. Over the years it has been known as 'Blind Billie', 'Blind Harrie' and 'Hoodle Cum Blind', but whatever you choose to call it, it's the way that you play it that counts.

Blindfold one player, revolve him a dozen times and let him go. His job is to catch any one of the sighted players — who are rushing and leaping and dodging out of his way — and guess that player's identity. If the Blind Man discovers the name of the player he has managed to catch, he and that player swap places.

Botticelli

One player thinks of the name of a famous person or a well-known fictitious character and reveals the first letter of his chosen subject's surname to the company, who must then try to find out who it is the player is thinking of.

They go about finding out by asking the player two types of question, indirect and direct. They can only ask a direct question if the player has failed to come up with a satisfactory answer to an indirect question. For example, if the player chooses to be Winston Churchill, he will announce 'I am someone beginning with C', and the others will proceed to fire indirect questions at him, such as 'Are you a French painter?', 'Are you a castaway?'. The player must reply along these lines: 'No, I am not Cezanne' or 'No, I am not Robinson Crusoe'. If he cannot think of appropriate answers, because he does not know of a French painter or a castaway beginning with C, or because his mind has gone blank at the crucial moment, the questioner can then ask a direct question ('Are you alive?', 'Are you fact?', 'Are you British?') to which a truthful 'yes' or 'no' answer must be given. It is important that the player chooses a character about whom he has some knowledge, or he may not be able to give correct answers to the direct questions.

Naturally, the questioners must do their best to ask awkward indirect questions in order to get as many opportunities as possible to put direct questions, which will lead them eventually to the secret identity they're after. The questioners can corner the player in one of two ways: either by asking an indirect question ('Were you born in 1874 and were you British Prime Minister between 1940 and 1945?'), which forces the player to reveal his identity, or by asking a direct question ('Are you Winston Churchill?') where the player has no alternative but to say 'Yes'.

Charades

Since 1776 Charades have been part of the British way of life. No party is complete without them and no man can call himself a true home entertainer unless he is a master of them.

As with all the great games the rules are simple. The players divide into teams and the first team disappears to another room to choose the word it is going to dramatise and to work out exactly how it is going to set about it. The word and the method having been decided upon, the captain of the team returns and announces to the rest of the company how many syllables there are in the word his team has chosen to dramatise and in what order these syllables are to be performed.

Various members of the team then come into the room and act, with or without dialogue (and it's far more entertaining without), a series of scenes designed to give clues to the sounds of the syllables they are dramatising, Each syllable is acted out individually and finally the word is performed as a whole. At the end of the performance the members of the audience have to guess the identity of the word.

A variation of traditional Charades that has become quite as popular as the original involves the performers in dramatising not simply an everyday word, but the name of a famous person, ship, town, country or mountain, or the title of a book, play, film or piece of music. And, as a further variation, if you do not have enough players to justify dividing into teams, you can play Solo Charades and get individuals to perform the words, names or titles of their choice all on their own.

And to get you going, here are some suggestions, all of which will lend themselves to dramatic interpretation, complete with a possible breakdown for each word in brackets:

abandon (a-ban-don)
ablution (a-blue-shone)
accustom (a-cus-tom)
acrostic (a-cross-tic)
albino (all-bean-no)
analysis (an-alley-sis)
answerable (an-sir-able)
antiquity (an-tic-witty)
aspirin (ass-peer-in)
automobile (auto-mob-ill)
barometer (barrow-meat-her)
bedevilment (bee-devil-mint)
blackamoor (black-amour)
blunderbuss (blunder-bus)
bouquet (boo-kay)
breastplate (breast-plate)
bulletin (bull-ate-in)
butterfly (but-her-fly)
byproduct (buy-prod-act)

bystander (by-stand-her)
cabbage (cab-age)
cabinet (cab-in-ate)
candidate (can-did-ate)
cantaloup (cant-a-loop)
capitalize (cap-it-all-lies)
carnival (car-navel)
cataract (catarrh-act)
chicken (chic-hen)
chieftain (chief-ten)
cucumber (queue-come-burr)
dainty (deign-tea)
decalogue (deck-her-log)
defrock (deaf-rock)
demanded (demon-dead)
determine (debt-ermine)
diversity (diver-city)
dogmatic (dog-mat-tic)
doldrums (doll-drums)

domesticity (dome-hasty-city)
donkey (don-key)
earthenware (earth-hen-wear)
electric (elect-trick)
emerald (hem-herald)
eskimo (s-scheme-oh)
esquire (s-choir)
eunuch (you-knock)
exactly (x-act-lie)
exchequer (x-check-her)
excursion (x-cur-shone)
execute (eggs-a-cute)
fantasy (fan-daisy)
farrago (far-ago)
fillip (fill-hip)
firmament (firm-am-meant)
flamboyant (flame-boy-ant)
foolhardy (fool-hard-d)
foreleg (four-leg)
forgotten (four-got-ten)
frigid (fridge-id)
fundamental (thunder-mental)
generalize (general-eyes)
genuine (gin-you-inn)
gospel (go-spell)
graceless (grace-less)
gravy (grave-e)
grocer (gross-sir)
guillotine (gill-low-teen)
gumption (gum-shone)
gymnasium (Jim-neighs-yum)
hallucination (hallo-sin-nation)
hammer (ham-her)
handkerchief (hanker-chief)
hardihood (hard-he-hood)
harvest (ha-vest)

horizon (whore-rise-son)
hospitality (horse-spit-alley-tea)
hundred (hun-dread)
hypnotic (hip-knot-tic)
ideal (eye-deal)
industry (in-dust-tree)
jabber (jab-her)
jackanapes (jack-Ann-apes)
jasmine (jazz-mine)
khaki (car-key)
letter (let-her)
lavatory (lava-tory)
liberate (lib-err-rate)
licorice (lick-core-is)
lieutenant (left-tenant)
Malaprop (mall-a-prop)
malcontent (mall-con-tent)
mangle (man-girl)
masterful (master-full)
metronome (met-row-gnome)
midsummer (mid-sum-her)
misunderstand (miss-under-stand)
molecular (mole-egg-queue-la)
mustard (must-hard)
number (numb-burr)
notwithstanding
  (not-with-standing)
perspex (purse-specs)
philanthropist
  (fill-and-throw-pissed)
physicist (fizz-is-cist)
redress (read-dress)
relate (reel-ate)
sacrament (sack-raiment)
sluggard (slug-hard)
tantamount (tan-ta-mount)

And here are some possible titles:
A Life on the Ocean Wave   *Great Expectations*
The Mill on the Floss   *Look Back in Anger*

Measure for Measure   Beauty and the Beast
Pride and Prejudice   What's My Line
My Fair Lady   I'm Dreaming of a White
The Go-between   Christmas
The Diary of a Nobody   A Woman of No Importance
School for Scandal   The Sting
Sergeant Pepper's Lonely Hearts   Goodbye Mr Chips
   Club Band   Midnight Cowboy
Rule Britannia   Pop Goes the Weasel

Cocktails

Give everyone a piece of paper and get them to write a series of categories down the left-hand margin of the page. If you are going to take the game seriously your categories might include:

rivers   saints   composers
flowers   mammals   birds
actors   statesmen   footballers
novels

And if you plan a more light-hearted (and actually rather more difficult) game, among the categories in your list might be:

famous divorcees   cocktails   sin cities
bad novels   sex kittens   poisons
criminals   restaurants   honeymoon resorts
honest millionaires

Once the categories have been listed, announce a letter of the alphabet chosen at random and give players a set time in which to list the name of a river, a flower, an actor, or whatever, beginning with the given letter. When the time is up, players read out their lists and score one point for every name listed by them *that no other player has listed*. As usual, the player with most points is the winner.

Consequences

Consequences, like Charades and Sardines and Blind Man's Buff, is a classic parlour game that has been played around the world for generations and yet still manages to retain its peculiar charm. To play it, equip everyone with a pencil and a long sheet of paper. Then tell the players to write down certain pieces of information and each time they have done so get them to fold the top of their pieces of paper forward (so that what they have written can't be seen) and pass the paper to the player sitting on their right. Gradually the pieces of information build up into a story and at the end of the game all the different stories are read out and the wittiest is given the warmest applause.

Traditionally a dozen pieces of information are called for, but you can add your own should you feel so inclined:

1. An adjective *(fold and pass)*.
2. A girl's name *(fold and pass)*.
3. The word MET plus an adjective *(fold and pass)*.
4. A man's name *(fold and pass)*.
5. The word AT plus details of where they met *(fold and pass)*.
6. When they met *(fold and pass)*.
7. The words HE SAID TO HER followed by what he said *(fold and pass)*.
8. The words SHE SAID TO HIM followed by what she said *(fold and pass)*.
9. What he then did *(fold and pass)*.
10. What she then did *(fold and pass)*.
11. The words AND THE CONSEQUENCE WAS plus details of the consequence *(fold and pass)*.
12. The words AND THE WORLD SAID plus details of what the world did say.

Constantinople

Give everyone a word — the longer the better — and a set time in which to write down the longest possible list of other words that can be formed with the letters in the original word. For example, the word *words* will give you *rod, sod, sow, row* and *sword*, for a start, and you will find words like the following contain twenty or more possible hidden words:

anonaceous	horoscopes	onomatopoeia	unreservedly
brontosaurus	intimidation	portmanteau	vibrations
characteristic	jointures	quadruplicate	wentletrap
domineering	loggerheads	ratiocinate	xylophone
effervescent	ministerial	seasonable	ytterbium
formidable	nomenclature	triumvirate	zucchetto
gargantuan			

At the end of the time limit, the player with the longest list of legitimate words is the winner.

Crambo

All the great masters of English literature — from Samuel Pepys to Virginia Woolf — have enjoyed the occasional game of Crambo. To play it, one player thinks of a word and announces a word that *rhymes* with the secret word he has thought of. The other players then have to guess the identity of the secret word by coming up with other words that will fit the rhyme. The players each have three attempts at guessing the word and the first player to get the answer is rewarded by being allowed to think of the next secret word.

A popular variation of the game is called Dumb Crambo. Here the players who are guessing the secret word don't announce what they think it might be: they *mime* what they consider to be the secret word! The sedentary will prefer Crambo but, for the eager, the energetic and the would-be Thespian, Dumbo Crambo is hard to beat.

Donkey

The aim of this world-famous word-game is to spell out words in a group and hopefully never be the player who finishes one. Players take it in turn to say a letter and each letter must go towards building up a proper word (three-letter words don't count). Since the players must have a definite word in mind before they announce their letters, a player can challenge the letter given by the preceding player if he cannot think of a word spelt in that particular way. Hapless players who finish words by saying the last letter, either inadvertently or because they have no alternative, and players who are challenged successfully having no particular word in mind, together with players who challenge others only to find that they did have legitimate words in mind, lose a life and once you've lost six lives you're a 'Donkey' and you're out.

Suppose there are three players and Player Number One begins with P (thinking of *party*), Player Number Two might follow with R (thinking of *practical*), Player Number Three could then come up with I (thinking of *prince*) and Player Number One would follow this with Z (because he is now thinking of *prize*), leaving Player Number Two with little alternative (because he thinks *prizing* is spelt with an S) but to say E and end the word and lose a life.

Hangman

This is a classic paper-and-pencil game for two players. To begin, one player thinks of a word of six, seven or eight letters and marks a dash for each letter, except in a couple of places where he gives letters as pointers. For example, if *bucket* was the word, it could be written out like this:

$$— — — K — T$$

Or like this:

$$— U C — — —$$

The opponent then tries to guess the remaining letters one by one, indicating the position for each letter as he names it. Every time he suggests the right letter for the right place, that letter is marked down. But every time he comes up with a letter that doesn't fit, the player who thought of the word is able to add an extra bit to his drawing of the gallows. The player who is doing the guessing has eleven lives to lose, in that the gallows consists of eleven gruesome parts:

1. The base of the gallows
2. The upright of the gallows
3. The arm of the gallows
4. The support
5. The rope
6. The victim's head
7. The victim's body
8. The victim's right arm
9. The victim's left arm
10. The victim's right leg
11. The victim's left leg

If the guesser comes up with the word before the gallows is complete, he has won. If he fails to he is hanged and has lost. The players then swap roles.

Leper, ring thy bell

In days when leprosy was common throughout Europe, this game was played for real. It involved children daring one another to run up to the local leper and taunt him. Fortunately that kind of cruelty is now almost an impossibility and today the game, for all its hateful history, can be allowed to provide innocent and uncomplicated amusement.

A Leper is chosen and given a small handbell. All the others are securely blindfolded. On the command 'Go', the Leper sets off around the house, moving about as he pleases, but pursued by the blind players who are supposed to do all they can to catch up with him. Whenever any of the blind pursuers calls out 'Leper, ring thy bell', the Leper must do just that. And the first player to catch hold of him takes his place.

Matchbox Race

To begin the game, divide the players into equal teams, getting each team to stand in line and giving the leader of each team the cover of a conventional matchbox. On the word 'Go', the leaders must push the matchbox covers over the ends of their noses, turn to the players next in line and attempt to transfer the boxes from their noses to the neighbouring noses. The players second in line must then pass the matchboxes on to the players third in line, and so it goes on. No hands are allowed and if a matchbox does fall to the ground it must be returned to the leader who replaces it on his own nose and starts all over again. The first team successfully to transfer its matchbox from one end of the line to the other wins.

Moriarty

Only two people can play this game at a time, but the bigger their audience the more fun will be had by all. The players are made to lie flat on their faces, opposite one another with their heads almost touching. They are blindfolded, made to grasp each other's left wrists with their left hands and each given a rolled-up newspaper to hold in their right hands.

On the command 'Go', the players take it in turn to call out 'Are you there, Moriarty?' and having heard a reply wallop each other. Each player gets an equal number of chances to put the question and at the end of the game the player with the greater number of direct hits is the winner. The skill, of course, lies in replying 'Yes' to the question in one place and then rolling quickly and quietly into another so that the newspaper blow misses entirely.

While nobody suggests that the distinguished detective, Sherlock Holmes, and his arch-enemy, Professor James Moriarty (after whom the game is named), ever set about each other with rolled-up newspapers, it is quite possible that Holmes and Dr Watson occasionally amused themselves with this sport to keep their spirits up during the quieter evenings in Baker Street.

Murder

A classic of its kind, this game is not recommended for people with weak hearts and nervous dispositions. No one is *known* to have died while playing it, but there can be little doubt that it has shortened one or two lives.

To begin, as many folded slips of paper as there are players are dropped into a hat. On one slip of paper a cross has been marked, on another a circle. All the other slips are blank. The player who draws the cross becomes the Murderer, but says nothing about it. The player who draws the circle becomes the Detective and declares himself. All the lights are then turned out and all the players, except the Detective, spread themselves about the house.

The Murderer, an evil glint in his eye, stalks about observing the shadowy figures of the other players. When he has chosen a victim, he pounces on him whispering in his ear, 'You're dead!'—whereupon the hapless victim screams for all he's worth and the Murder steals stealthily away.

The moment he hears the scream, the Detective rushes towards the scene of the crime, switching on all the lights as he goes. And from the moment the scream is heard all the players, excepting the Murderer, must stand stock still. The Detective then observes the positions and attitudes of the different players and questions them in turn. All the players, again excepting the murderer, must answer truthfully. The Murderer, of course, can tell any lies he likes, except when he is eventually asked the direct question 'Are you the Murderer?' when he must make a complete confession. The Detective can only ask the direct question twice and if he has failed to discover the brute whodunnit, the murderer then steps forward to take a bow.

Nostrils

This game requires a few moments preparation. Before the players appear, place half a dozen or more glasses on a tray and fill each one with a different liquid. Be sure they all have distinct flavours because the aim of the game is to test the players' nostrils. When the tray is ready, blindfold all the players and lead them up to it in turn. Each player sniffs at every glass and then goes away to write down what he thinks the contents might be. The player with the most accurate list is the winner—and, if you're kind, you allow him to drink the glasses containing the wine and cocoa. The player with the least accurate list is the loser—and, if you're unkind, you make him drink the glasses containing the custard and washing-up liquid!

O'Grady says

One player is chosen to play the part of O'Grady. He stands facing all the others and barks a whole succession of commands at them. Whenever he says 'O'Grady says do such-and-such', the players must obey. But when he doesn't mention his own name and simply says 'Do such-and-such', the players must *not* obey him. Anyone caught obeying an order not prefaced by the words 'O'Grady says', drops out. The last player left obeying the commands is the winner.

The idea is that when the leader says 'O'Grady says touch your toes', you do it, and when he says 'O'Grady says put your hands on your hips', you do it, but when he shouts 'Fold your arms', you don't.

A famous variation of the game involves the leader demonstrating various gestures to the other players and saying as he does so 'Do this' or 'Do that'. When he says 'Do this', the players must do it. But when he says 'Do that' they most emphatically must not.

One-minute Walk

Confiscate all the watches and cover up all the clocks. Then line your players along one side of the room and tell them to cross to the other side in precisely sixty seconds. They can travel at any speed they like, but they mustn't stop moving. Players who do come to a halt or who reach the other side before the time is up are out. The player who is nearest the other side at the very moment the minute is up is, of course, the winner.

Pan tapping

While one player is sent out of the room, all the others decide on an unlikely task for him to perform on his return. It might be that he has got to take a picture off the wall or pick a flower from the vase and tuck it behind his ear or kiss his hostess on the nose. Whatever it is, when he returns he is encouraged by one of the other players who has been equipped with a saucepan and a wooden spoon and is supposed to act as his guide. When the outsider moves towards the object he has to touch, say the picture he must take off the wall, the guide taps loud and fast on the saucepan. When the outsider moves away from the object, the guide taps slow and soft. The nearer the outsider gets to the object, and what he has to do with it or to it, the more furious is the pan-tapping, and the game goes on until the outsider has performed his task or his guide has collapsed from exhaustion—when it becomes another player's turn to leave the room.

Party Alibi

Not many parlour games spring from the 1930s, but this is one that does. It involves two players accused of a heinous crime and their attempt to defend themselves with a hopefully watertight alibi. The players are invited to leave the room and are given ten minutes in which to concoct their alibi. They must pretend they were together for three whole hours—the three hours during which the dreadful crime was perpetrated—and must agree between themselves as to exactly what happened to both of them throughout that time.

Once they have settled on their story, one of them is brought back into the room and questioned closely by the assembled company for five minutes. They can ask him anything they like about his activities during the tell-tale one-hundred-and-eighty minutes and he must come up with an answer to all their questions. When they have finished with Suspect Number One, Suspect Number Two is brought in for questioning.

The aim of the game, of course, is to break the two players' alibi by making Suspect Number Two say something that does not tally with whatever Suspect Number One has already said. If there are no discrepancies discovered between the stories, the suspects are released and congratulated. However, if Suspect Number Two fails to corroborate Suspect Number One's story, the unhappy pair are found guilty and condemned.

Pass the Orange

Get all the players to stand in a circle and attempt to pass an orange from one to another holding the beastly fruit underneath their chins. No hands are allowed and any player dropping the orange or caught trying to transfer it other than by using his chin and shoulders must leave the circle.

As a variation on the traditional game, you can always try passing the orange from knee to knee, with the players holding the fruit between their knees and keeping their arms folded behind their backs. It isn't easy and played by those with knobbly knees can be extremely painful.

Postman's Knock

It is its very innocence which gives this game its charm. To play it you need at least six players, and half of them should be men or boys and the other half women or girls. To begin, one of the men leaves the room, while the other players give themselves numbers — even numbers for the men, uneven for the women. When all the players have their numbers, they call out 'We're ready!' and the outsider knocks firmly on the door, 'Who is it?' shout all the players. 'Tis I, the postman,' comes the reply, 'and I have something here for Number Three (or One or Five or Seven or Nine or any other uneven number). Will you come and get it?'

At this point Number Three has to go out and join the postman who gives her a kiss — much, hopefully, to his and her delight. The pair then return to the room and it becomes the turn of another player — a girl this time — to go out. New numbers are chosen and the whole process is repeated when the postman (or, in this case, postmistress) knocks.

The Railway Carriage Game

Two players are chosen and each of them is given a secret (and slightly absurd) phrase, sentence or expression. For example, Player Number One's phrase could be 'Pop goes the weasel!' while Player Number Two's phrase might be 'Holy mackerel!' Armed with their phrases, the players must climb into an imaginary railway carriage and chat to one another for the length of a five-minute journey. During the course of their conversation each player must slip his or her secret phrase into whatever he or she happens to say. It isn't easy — particularly when you remember that the aim of the game is to say your secret phrase without your travelling companion realising you've said it.

When the journey is over, Player Number One must guess the identity of Player Number Two's phrase and vice-versa.

Sardines

Alive, sardines never play this game. Dead, they have little alternative. Get all the players together in one room and release them one by one at two or three minute intervals. The first player to set out must find a good spot to hide and the players that set out after him must attempt to find his hideout and join him in it. Naturally, by the time all the players have discovered the original player and joined him in the attic or the larder or the outside lavatory or the cubby-hole under the stairs, they are fairly tightly packed in — like sardines, in fact.

Of all Victorian parlour games, this was one of the most popular. Alas, played in an age of bed-sitting rooms and box flats it loses much of the charm that it had in the heyday of fine town houses and magnificent mansions. All the same, while it has to be scaled down for the last quarter of the twentieth century, as games go it remains a classic of its kind.

Taboo

An everyday word—like 'I' or 'and' or 'the' or 'this' or 'that'—is declared taboo and must not be spoken by any of the players. The leader of the group questions each player in turn and any player uttering the fatal word drops out. The last player left answering questions is the winner. To make the game more complex, you can ban a particular letter of the alphabet and all words containing that letter are then taboo.

Tennis elbow foot

The players form a circle and take it in turn to call out words that are *either* directly related to the last word called out *or* rhyme with it. For example, the first three rounds of the game, played by four players, might go like this:

Player 1: *tennis*	Player 1: *sweep*	Player 1: *town*
Player 2: *elbow*	Player 2: *chimney*	Player 2: *city*
Player 3: *foot*	Player 3: *top*	Player 3: *pity*
Player 4: *soot*	Player 4: *toy*	Player 4: *gritty*

Players drop out if they hesitate or come out with a word that doesn't really relate to the previous word or doesn't actually rhyme with it. The last player left talking is the winner.

Toes

It is almost impossible to imagine the Victorians playing this game, but they apparently did—and with gusto. The players have to divide into teams and, while one team is sent from the room members of the other team proceed to remove their shoes, slippers, socks, stockings and tights. Barefooted they then stand behind a screen or, better still, lie on the floor covered from head to ankle by a large sheet. Whichever way it's done, in the end all that should be seen is a row of feet.

The members of the team that left the room now return and, resisting the temptations to tickle the row of toes displayed before them, must attempt to work out which feet belong to which player. When the team has agreed on what tops go with which toes, the screen or sheet is removed and the guessers can see how right or wrong they were.

This is a glorious game for all the family, excepting those suffering from athlete's foot and verrucas.

Treasure Hunt

In Victorian and Edwardian days no party was ever complete without a Treasure Hunt. Of course, the parlour game-playing English gentry of yesteryear did tend to have splendid rambling mansions, ideally suited to a tense Treasure Hunt, while most modern home entertainers must make do with pokey flats and pint-sized semis. Whatever the location for this game, to play it requires a little homework. Before the players set out to hunt the treasure, it's got to be hidden. And once it's hidden, ingenious clues have got to be laid along the route leading to it.

To make the hunt a success, it's important to remember that the clues should be ingenious but not impossible and that the treasure should consist of something truly worth finding. If it isn't, the game ends on a saddening note of anticlimax.

Twenty Questions

One player thinks of an object — it can be anything from the Eiffel Tower to a parson's nose — and tells all the other players whether it is animal, vegetable, mineral or a combination of all three. The others then fire questions, requiring only 'Yes' or 'No' answers and aimed at narrowing the field and at eventually closing in on the object. Only twenty questions are allowed and the player who is thinking of the object has won if, once all twenty questions have been answered, the other players still haven't guessed the identity of the mystery object.

Virginia Woolf

All the players have to think of the person they would most like to be if they couldn't be themselves. You can choose to be a character from fact or fiction, alive or dead, male or female, but you should be someone whose name people are likely to know.

When everyone has chosen his or her ideal identity, each player takes it in turn to be quizzed by the remaining players who are aiming to find out who the player in question wants to be. Twenty questions are allowed, requiring either 'Yes' or 'No' answers, and when the secret identity has been revealed the player whose choice it was must explain *why* he wanted to be whoever it was he happened to choose.

Winking

A classic of its kind, this game should not be played by people with natural nervous twitches. They will only confuse the issue. To play the game, form a circle of inward-facing chairs and place a girl in each chair, except one which is left empty. Behind each chair, including the empty one, stands a man with his hands resting on the top of the chair, but not actually touching the girl sitting in it.

The man standing behind the empty chair starts the game by *winking* at any one of the other girls who must attempt to leave her chair and rush to his. Naturally, the man standing behind her must try to stop her from going by putting his hands on her shoulders. If he's quick enough, the girl must stay where she is and the winker must wink at somebody else. If she manages to get away, it becomes the turn of the man who has been deserted to do the winking.

Once all the girls have been winked at, change over and let the women do the winking.

2. DO-IT-YOURSELF BOARD GAMING

From Persepolis in Persia to Poole in Dorset, men, women and children have been playing these board games for hundreds of years. Though they come from a dozen different countries, the rules are all simple to learn, and though half of them are manufactured commercially, the boards and pieces are all easy to make. For counters you can use buttons or coins or bottle-tops, or even gambling chips or slices of raw carrot or shells. And for the boards, all you need are a few large sheets of paper and one, or at most two, coloured pencils or pens.

Achi

Related to Alquerque and Madelinette, to Nine Men's Morris and Noughts and Crosses, Achi is one of the world's most ancient board

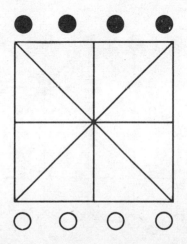

Achi board

games. Almost unknown today in Europe, it is still played throughout Africa, most enthusiastically in Ghana, where it is very nearly the national sport.

Two players, with four counters each, sit either side of a simple board looking something like that shown on the previous page.

The players toss to see who begins and then take alternate turns. They start by putting each of their four counters on to different points on the board. Placing the eight counters takes up the first eight moves. Then the action begins, as the players move one counter at a time along a line to another free point in an attempt to get three in a row.

The first player who manages to manoeuvre his counters so as to get three in a row is the winner.

Alquerque

Characters like Alfonso X of Spain didn't have television, and they didn't have radio. They didn't even have Monopoly. But their lives weren't unendurably dull because they did have amusements of their own and Alquerque was one of them. It's a board game for two players that was invented in the tenth century, enjoyed a great vogue in the thirteenth, but hasn't been much heard of since.

The players toss to see who begins and armed with twelve counters each — two different sorts of button or coin or bottle-top will do — they play on a board looking something like this:

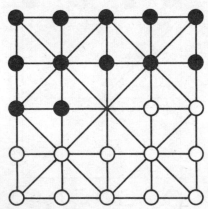

Alquerque board

The players have alternate moves and the counters can be moved from any point to any adjacent point along a line. If the adjacent point is occupied by one of the enemy's counters and the next point beyond it on the line is empty, the player's counter may make a short jump over the enemy's counter which is then removed from the board. If another enemy counter is now at risk, it too can be taken in the same move by a second short leap, whether or not this involves a change of direction. Any number of counters can be captured like this in any one move.

It is crucial to remember that if a counter can capture an enemy's counter *it must do so*. If it fails to do so, then the enemy will huff it — which, translated from the gamesman's jargon, means claim it as a forfeit — and remove it from the board.

When one player has lost all his counters, his opponent has won the game.

Draughts

In Poland, Spain, Turkey and France they play Draughts in their own original ways. In Britain and in America (where they call it Checkers) we play it this way — the best way and, in the eyes of some, the *only* way.

You need two players, twenty-four counters (traditionally they are flat round slices of wood, twelve white and twelve black) and a chess board. When the counters are in position the board should look something like this:

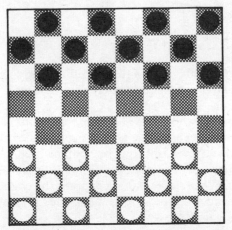

Draughts board

To work out who has the black counters and who the white, one of the players takes a counter of each colour and clenches one in each fist. His opponent chooses a fist and has to play with the colour of the counter contained in the fist. Black always moves first.

The game is played on the black squares, which means that the counters move diagonally to the left or right. The counters can only move one square at a time and can only move forward. However, once a counter reaches one of the four squares on the far side of the board, it becomes a King and can move forwards *and* backwards. For easy identification Kings are usually crowned with a second counter and travel about the board as double-deckers.

The aim of the game is to capture all your opponent's counters, or at least to block them so that they can't move, and to capture a counter you must jump over it. Remember, of course, that counters can only move on to squares that are empty, but that to get to an empty square they can jump over their own as well as their opponent's counters. Indeed, if a counter is in a position to jump over an enemy's counter it *must* do so, and as many times as possible, because by jumping over different counters in succession you can capture any number. If you fail to capture an enemy's counter when given the chance, you will be huffed — which means that the enemy can take the man (or King) who failed to jump when he had the opportunity, or can oblige you to take back your last move. It is then his turn. The first player to block his opponent or capture all his counters wins.

Four Field Kono

The Koreans invented this simple but compelling board game. Only two can play and each player has eight counters arranged on a board to look something like the one illustrated.

The players toss to see who starts and then make alternate moves, the aim of the game being to capture the enemy's counters or at least to hem them in. The counters do their capturing by jumping over one of their own counters and landing on an enemy counter standing on a point immediately beyond. When not making a capture the counters can move along the lines one point at a time. The winner is the first player to capture or block the enemy's troops.

Four Field Kono board

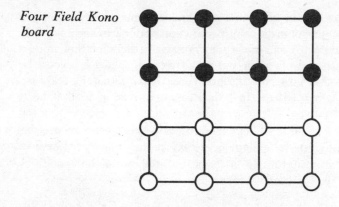

Fox and Geese

King Edward IV had hidden depths that the history books rarely plumb. After all, did you know that Fox and Geese was one of his favourite games and that he rarely stopped boasting about his superb set of 'two foxis and twenty-six hounds of silver overgilt'?

While Edward IV used hounds rather than geese in his version of the game and was wealthy enough to be able to afford two sets of pieces for the game, to play it today all you need are one fox (a coin will do) and thirteen geese (buttons will do) laid out on a board looking something like this:

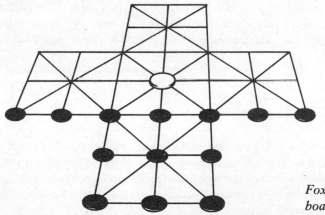

Fox and Geese board

Two players take part in this game and one becomes the fox while the other herds the geese. As usual, you toss to see who starts and take it in turns to play. Both the fox and the geese can move in any direction along a line to a neighbouring empty point, but if the fox can jump over a goose he is allowed to take that goose off the board and have him for breakfast. While the geese cannot eat the fox, they can hem him in so that he is unable to move.

The fox wins the game if he manages to eat enough geese to prevent them from hemming him in and the geese win if they manage to hem in the fox. The odds are definitely in favour of the geese, but you'll be surprised how very crafty many foxes can be.

Grasshopper

To play this game you need a chess board of the sort illustrated in the description of the game of Draughts earlier on. You also need two players with ten counters each. The counters are laid out in opposite corners of the board, on the black and white squares, in four diagonal rows, with one counter in the corner square, two in a line parallel to that, three in a line parallel to that, and four in the last line parallel to that.

The object of the exercise is to get all your counters from your corner across into your opponent's corner. He will be trying to do the same thing and the first of you to make it is the winner. You move the counters one at a time on to empty squares. You can jump other counters (yours or your opponent's) providing you can land on an empty square immediately beyond the counter you've just hopped. And in any one move you can jump over a number of counters, providing each time you can land on an empty square.

Horseshoe

All you need for this game are two players and a pair of counters for each of them. The board is very simple (and unusual since it actually has some connection with the name of the game and looks a little like a horseshoe) and once the players' pieces are in position it will look something like this:

Horseshoe board

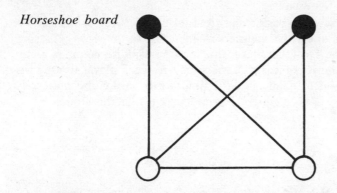

The players toss to see who starts and then take it in turns to move. The first player moves one of his counters along a line to the empty crossing point in the middle. The other player then moves one of his pieces along a line to the new empty point. And so this goes on, each player moving one of his counters at a time, until one of the players is unable to move either of his counters. His opponent has then won.

Madelinette

The principle of Madelinette is identical to that of Horseshoe, but the game has more to it because each of the two players has three counters and the board is a touch more complex, looking at the outset something like this:

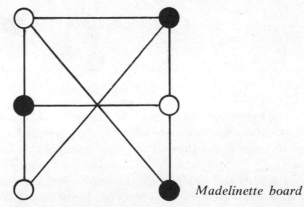

Madelinette board

Players toss to see who begins and then take it in turns to move. The first player moves one of his counters along a line to the empty crossing point in the middle. The other player then moves one of his counters along a line to the new empty point. This carries on, with each player moving his counters from point to point one at a time, until one of the players is unable to move any of his counters. His opponent is then the winner.

Mu-torere

The Maoris of New Zealand have given this game to the world. Two players take part, each armed with four pieces which they place on four adjacent points of an eight-pointed star looking something like this:

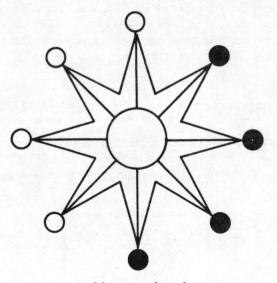

Mu-torere board

The Maoris call the circle in the centre the *putahi* and the circles on the ends of the arms, where the counters are positioned, are called *kewai*.

The aim of the game is to make it impossible for your opponent to move.

The rules are simple: a counter can be moved from one of the *kewai* to the next, if it is empty; a counter can also be moved from one of the *kewai* to the *putahi* but *only* if one of the *kewai* next to it (or both of them for that matter) has one of the enemy's counters on it; finally a counter can always be moved from the *putahi* to one of the empty *kewai*.

The first player to block his opponent wins.

Nine Holes

The hairy Ainus of Japan played this game. So did the high priests of Ancient Greece. So did the Arab warriors. So do English choirboys. We can be quite sure about the choirboys because the evidence is there for all to see. You can visit any number of English cathedrals and there, as likely as not, you will find a Nine Holes board scratched into the cloister seats.

The board looks like this:

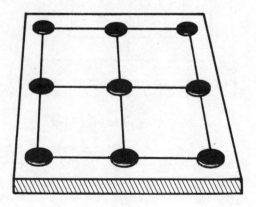

Nine Holes board

Only two players can take part and each one starts with three counters — or coins or shells or buttons or bottle-tops. Players take it in turns to move and toss to see who begins. The first six moves are used for positioning the counters. Once in place, a player can move any one of his counters along one of the lines to an adjacent empty space.

The aim of the game is to make a row of three and the first player who manages it is the winner.

Nine Men's Morris

Nine Men's Morris is one of the oldest board games of them all. The board has been found scratched on to a stone from a Bronze Age burial plot in Ireland, on to part of the roof of a 3,500-year-old monument in Egypt and on to the steps of an ancient temple in Ceylon. Scratched on to wood, chalked on to a paving stone or simply drawn on to a piece of paper, this is how the board should look:

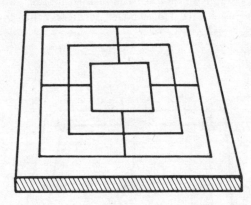

Nine Men's Morris board

Again this is a game for just two players, each of them equipped with nine individual counters, and, as usual, they toss to see who starts. They then take it in turns to place their counters on empty points on the board. The aim as they do this is to make a row of three along any one line. Whenever a player succeeds in doing this, as his reward he is allowed to remove one of his enemy's counters from the board.

Once all the counters have been placed on the board, the players move their counters, one at a time and a single jump at a time to an empty neighbouring point, the aim still being to make a row of three. A row of three can always be broken by moving a counter out and then remade by moving it back next turn. Whether the row is being made for the first time or is being remade, the player who makes it can claim a counter from his enemy each time.

Naturally, the player who captures so many of his enemy's counters that the enemy cannot any longer make a row of three, or the player who blocks his enemy's men so that none of them can be moved, is the winner.

Noughts and Crosses

It has been suggested, but never proved, that this game is known by more people on the face of the earth than any other. Certainly it has been around since the Middle Ages (when it was commonly known as Three Men's Morris) and doubtless it will survive this century and live to entertain future generations.

Two players take part and they begin by drawing a grid of nine squares, with three squares in each row. The first player puts a nought (looking like the letter O) in any one of the nine squares. The opponent then puts a cross (looking like the letter X) in any of the eight remaining squares. This carries on, with one player placing noughts while the other places crosses, until one player has managed to get three noughts or three crosses in a row (vertically, horizontally, or diagonally) or until all the squares have been filled in.

The first player to get three in a row is the winner. If no one manages to make a row, the game is a draw and you start all over again.

Reversi

Reversi, a board game invented in the 1880s, was one of the most popular pastimes of the late Victorian period. All you need to play Reversi is a chess board (with sixty-four squares) and sixty-four counters, which are black on one side and white on the other.

One player is Black, the other White, and Black begins by placing one of his thirty-two counters black-side up on one of the four central squares of the empty board. White then places his first piece white-side up on another central square. The four central squares are covered in the first four moves of the game and then the players carry on, moving alternately and placing their counters on any square adjacent to one occupied by an enemy's counter.

In making this move a player may 'trap' one of the enemy's counters:
that is to say, if Black puts a counter adjacent to a counter of White's that
already has a black counter adjacent to it, Black has trapped the white
counter that now lies between the two black counters. Any enemy counters
that lie between a counter just played and another counter of the player's
own colour, whether the line is diagonal, horizontal or vertical, are
captured in this way and are turned over to display the player's colour
topside uppermost. For example, if Black manages to trap one of White's
counters, the counter he has trapped is reversed and becomes a black one.
Counters can change owners (and colours) numerous times in the course
of a game.

The winner is the player who has the greater number of counters of his
colour on display after the sixty-fourth counter has been placed on the
board.

Solitaire

In the jet-set age the game of Solitaire has become an 'executive toy'
and no flashy advertising director's office is complete unless its
furnishings include a swish Solitaire set, created in stainless steel and
polished ebony. Humbler folk can simply draw a Solitaire board of their
own. All they need to do is to mark thirty-three dots on a piece of paper
like this:

Solitaire board.

Now place thirty-two little objects (halfpennies, drawing pins, postage stamps) on any thirty-two of the thirty-three dots. These objects can only move by jumping over another object on to an empty dot. The jumps can be horizontal, vertical or diagonal, but you can only jump over one object at a time. Any objects which are jumped over are taken off the board.

The aim of the game, which you play on your own, is to end up with just *one* object left on the board. And if you want to make life really difficult for yourself, you can decide before you start *where* that one object is eventually going to be positioned.

Treasure Trove

Two players, two pencils, one piece of paper and one umpire are all you need for this game. The umpire begins by drawing a grid of eighty-one squares (nine across and nine down) and by marking the numbers 1 to 9 at the top of the vertical column and the letters A to I at the side of the horizontal column. He then secretly allocates four of the nine letters A, B, C, D, E, F, G, H and I, and four of the nine numbers, 1, 2, 3, 4, 5, 6, 7, 8 and 9, to one player and four others to the other player. Neither player must know what four letters and four numbers his opponent has been given, nor must he know which letter and which number have been left over.

The one letter and one number that are *not* allocated identify a particular square on the board — and it's that square that hides the buried treasure. The first player to find the square is the winner.

The players toss to see who begins and in his turn a player can do one of two things: he can *either* ask his opponent if he holds a certain letter or number (and while the opponent must reply truthfully it is quite in order for a player to ask an opponent if he happens to have a letter or number he himself has in order to confuse the opponent and make him think that that letter or number may indicate the column in which the treasure is to be found), *or* he can suggest the actual position of the treasure, in which case if he is correct he wins the game but if he is not and his opponent holds either the specified letter or number or both the opponent simply says 'You're wrong' and takes his turn.

Wari

A seventeenth-century Livingstone was probably the first man to bring word of Wari back to Europe from Africa. He noted in his diary, 'In the heat of the day the men will come forth and sit under shady trees to receive fresh air, and there pass the time, having only one kind of game, and that is in a peece of wood with great holes cut, which they set betwixt two of them, with some thirty pibble stones. They take one from the other until one is possessed of all whereat some of them are wondrous nimble.'

Nimble or not, to play the game today you need twelve saucers and forty-eight seeds (buttons or pebbles or halfpennies will do just as well). Lay out the twelve saucers in two rows, with six saucers in each row, and place four of the seeds in each saucer.

There are two players and they sit opposite each other with the two rows of saucers between them. Whoever has won the toss and is to start begins by taking all the seeds from any one saucer in his row and sowing them *anti-clockwise* one by one in each of the four neighbouring saucers. If the sowing leads him to the end of his row he carries on to his opponent's row sowing the seeds in his saucers.

When the first player has sown all four seeds, the opponent has his turn and sows all the seeds from any one of his saucers. The first player then sows again, and so the game continues. Naturally, if a saucer contains twelve or more seeds the sowing from it will take more than one complete circle of the saucers, in which case the original saucer from which the twelve or more seeds came is left empty and remains empty until the end of the game.

If the last seed from any particular sowing falls into a saucer already containing one or two seeds, the sower wins *all* the seeds in that saucer and takes them off the board. He also captures the seeds in any of the adjacent saucers that happen to contain exacly two or three seeds.

The winner is the player who ends up with most seeds. If there are only a few seeds left in the saucers, it may be that no more seed captures are possible, in which case the game stops and the seeds are counted. The game also stops when a player's saucers are empty and he has no seeds to sow when it comes to his turn. However, when an opponent's saucers are empty, a player must if at all possible make a sowing which will place seeds into his opponent's saucers. If he cannot the game is definitely over and he keeps all the seeds on the board as well as the ones he has already captured.

3. FUN WITH CARDS

It is amazing what you can do with the numbers one to thirteen when you have got four sets of them. For a start, you can call them playing cards and armed with a pack you can not only tell fortunes and lose fortunes, but also entertain yourself and your family and friends for hour upon hour.

This chapter contains nine forms of patience, ten card-games for two or more and ten card-tricks. With none of them will you have to struggle with the rules. The more serious card-games — the ones that people go to school to learn about and develop hernias playing — and the more complicated card-tricks — the ones that require sleight of hand, years of practice and full membership of the Magic Circle — have *not* been included, because the object of the exercise is not to start anybody off on a course of earnest study, but to give everybody easy access to thirty different ways of having fun with cards.

All Elevens
Patience

From a complete pack of cards deal nine and lay them out face upwards in three rows of three. Count the 'pips' (as playing-cards buffs call the emblems on the cards that indicate their value) and if any two cards total eleven — as would an Ace and a Ten or a Four and a Seven or a Three and an Eight — deal two new cards and place them on top of them.

In this patience, Kings and Queens and Knaves don't count, so if one happens to turn up you can deal another card and cover it. You can also deal a new card and put it on the card in the middle, when no two of the cards add up to eleven and no Kings, Queens or Knaves are on display.

The aim of the game is to be able to deal out all the cards, but if you've covered up all the cards that added up to eleven, covered up all the court cards in sight *and* covered up the cards in the middle, yet still cannot make eleven, you've lost. It's tough.

The Carpet
Patience

Deal twenty cards and lay them face upwards in four rows, with five cards in each row. This is the Carpet. If any Aces turn up as you are forming the Carpet, lay them to one side where they will form the bases for four sequences to be built up from Ace to King in the appropriate suit. If any Twos appear while the Carpet is under construction, they can be placed on top of the Aces of their suit, as can Threes, Fours, Fives and all, so long as you don't deviate from the suit-sequence.

When the Carpet is complete, you can deal all the remaining cards face upwards into a spare heap, removing the top card whenever it happens to be one that will fit on to one of the four Ace-based columns. Whenever a gap occurs in the Carpet, it should be filled if possible from the cards in the spare heap, but if all the cards in the spare heap have been placed on Ace-based columns, then the gap in the Carpet can be filled with a card dealt from the pack.

You can only go through the pack once, by which time, with a lot of luck, you should have four complete columns running from Ace to King, and no Carpet. If that's the case, you've won. If it isn't, you lose.

Doubles or Quits
Patience

Deal thirty-six cards face downwards into twelve heaps, with three cards in each heap. Now place one card face upwards on top of each of the twelve heaps. Look at these exposed cards, sort out the pairs and remove them from the game. Turn up the cards lying underneath the ones that have been paired off and, when possible, pair these off as well. If a gap appears because all four cards in any one heap have been paired off, fill the gap with one of the four cards that remain undealt.

When you have used up the four cards, continue pairing off until you can go no further. If you pair off all the cards in the pack you have won; if some remained unpaired, you have lost.

Great Aunt's Patience
Patience

Deal the cards into seven columns: the left-hand column must contain six cards face down and a seventh card face up, the second column must contain five cards face down and one face up, the third column four cards face down and one face up, and so on up to the seventh (and final) column which consists of just one card face up. If any of the exposed cards is an Ace, put that Ace aside where it will form the base of an ascending pile following suit-sequence from Ace to King. You can also place any exposed Twos, Threes and so on, on top of the Aces of the appropriate suit.

Now that the cards have been dealt and any Aces removed, sort the exposed cards into descending sequences of alternate colours. For example, if a black Eight and a red Nine are exposed, place the Eight on the Nine. Turn up the bottom card in those columns from which exposed cards have been taken and continue sorting.

When no more sorting is possible, deal the remaining cards in threes into a spare heap face upwards. When the top card on the spare heap can be placed on one of the seven columns, or on one of the Ace-based piles, do so. If a gap occurs among the seven columns, it can be filled with an exposed King from one of the other columns or from the top of the exposed heap.

You can only go through the spare heap once. The object of the patience is to build up the Ace-based columns from Ace to King. (You can cheat by going through the spare heap twice.)

Kings and Queens
Patience

Deal out the whole pack face upwards into four heaps, removing the Aces as they appear and placing them in a row above the heaps and removing the Twos as they appear and placing them in a row below the heaps. These eight cards will form the bases for eight columns to be built up in ascending order with alternating numbers and alternating colours — so a red Ace must be followed by a black Three which must be followed by a red Five and so on, and a red Two must be followed by a black Four which must be followed by a red Six and so on. To make the patience work you must end up with the Kings at the top of the Ace-based columns and the Queens at the top of the Two-based columns. It sounds simple, but as so often in patience you can only go through the pack once, and it isn't easy.

Patient Snap
Patience

The aim of the game is to turn over every card in the pack while calling out its name and *not* have any card come up as you are calling it. The idea is that as you turn over the first card, you call 'Ace'. If it *is* an Ace, you've lost the patience and that's that. If it isn't you can carry, on, turning over the next card and calling 'Two'. If card number two happens to be a Two, you've lost again, but if it turns out to be anything but a Two you can continue, until you've got safely passed the Ten, Knave, Queen and King when you start again with Ace. You have triumphed if you succeed in turning over all fifty-two cards in the pack.

Red Ace, Black Deuce
Patience

From a complete pack remove the Ace of Hearts, the King of Clubs, the Ace of Diamonds and the King of Spades and put them in a row in that order. Those four cards will form the bases of four columns, to be built upwards from the two Aces and downwards from the two Kings in a sequence of alternating colours. In this way a red Ace will be followed by a black Deuce (which is what card snobs call a Two), and a black King will be followed by a red Queen, and the Ace columns will culminate with red Kings while the King columns will culminate with black Aces.

To play the patience you deal out the remaining forty-eight cards into four piles, picking out cards to place on the columns when they occur in the correct sequence. Having dealt all forty-eight cards once, you gather the four piles together again and deal them into another four piles, picking out cards that fit on to the columns as and when you come to them.

By the time you have been through the pack for the second time in this way, you should have completed your columns. If you have, you've won. If you haven't you've lost.

Sir Tommy
Patience

Though members of the British Playing Cards Society might dispute it, the fact that Sir Tommy is one of the oldest forms of patience — if not *the* oldest form — cannot be denied. To play, all you do is build up four columns of cards, from the Aces to the Kings, not according to suit, but simply in the ascending order. You can only go through the pack once, so when you come to play you've got to concentrate. Simply deal out the cards into four piles, removing the Aces as they turn up and piling the Twos, Threes, Fours, Fives and so on, on top of them as they appear. As you will find when you try it, it's far more enthralling — and infuriating! — than it sounds.

Thirteen plus
Patience

Deal the whole pack into thirteen piles, with four cards in each pile, all of them face upwards. Now count pips on the exposed cards — remembering that Aces count as one, Knaves as eleven, Queens as twelve and Kings as thirteen — and hope that they total ninety-one. If they do, you've won already, because the aim of the game is to make the thirteen exposed cards total precisely ninety-one. If they don't (which is more than likely), you can move any number of top cards from one heap to another, providing that you always retain thirteen heaps.

There are scores of possible ways of achieving the magical total of ninety-one, but the most obvious, though one of the most difficult to achieve, calls for a complete sequence of cards through from Ace to King. If you want to make the patience doubly difficult, set that as your target.

Beggar My Neighbour
Card-game for two or more

Like Snap, Cheat and Old Maid, Beggar My Neighbour belongs to that select circle of classic parlour card-games that evoke all that is best about home entertainment. It's a fast game, it's a funny game, it's easy to learn and anyone can play it.

Begin by dividing the cards between the players face downwards. Players then take it in turns to deal one card at a time and put it in a pile in the middle of the table. This continues until one of the players turns up a Knave, Queen, King or Ace. When a player turns up a court card, the next player must play one or more penalty cards and the player who came up with the court card gets all the cards so far played and returns them to his hand. The penalties are straightforward: when a Knave turns up the next player must cover it with one card, when a Queen with two cards, when a King with three cards, when an Ace with four cards. But the player paying the penalty stops turning up these penalty cards if one of them turns out to be either a Knave, Queen, King or Ace — when it becomes the next player's turn to cover the Knave, Queen, King or Ace with one, two, three or four cards. This goes on until one of the players has paid a penalty in full without turning up a court card, in which case the last player to have played a court card is the one which picks up the whole pile and joins it to the cards still in his hand.

The player who ends up with all the cards in the pack is the winner.

Black Maria
Card-game for three

Begin by removing the Two of Clubs from the pack and deal seventeen cards face downwards to each of the players. When the players have studied their cards they pass three of them face downward to the player sitting on their left. No player may look at the cards he is about to receive until he has passed on the ones he has chosen to discard. When play begins, the aim of the game is *not* to win any tricks containing any Hearts, or the Ace, King and Queen of Spades, because these cards carry penalty points and at the end of a set number of rounds the player with the least number of penalty points is the winner and the player with the most is the loser. All the Hearts count as one point, the Ace of Spades counts as seven, the King of Spades as ten and the Queen of Spades (old Black Maria herself) as thirteen points.

As usual, the player to the left of the dealer plays first; other players must follow suit when they can; Aces are high and there are no trumps.

The game can be played with four players by using the full pack.

Bromsgrove
Card-game for three or more

If you have three players, just play with the Aces, Twos and Threes. If you have four, add the Fours, if five the Fives, if six the Sixes, and so on. Shuffle the cards and deal four to each player. As soon as the cards have been dealt, each player quickly sorts them and passes one card on to the player on his left. At the same time, of course, he accepts a card from the player on his right. This carries on — players passing to the left and accepting from the right — until one of the players finds he has four cards of a kind in his hand when he lays them gently on the table and folds his arms. As soon as the other players notice, they follow suit, and the last player to have folded his arms is the loser.

Cheat
Card-game for two or more

Cheat is a thrilling game, as subtle as bridge, wilder than pontoon, cheaper than poker. Once the cards have been dealt, the first player to the left of the dealer who holds an Ace places it on the table face downwards and says 'Ace' as he does so. The next player must place a second card on top of the Ace and say 'Two'. The third player must now cover the second card and say 'Three'. This is how the game progresses, with the players putting cards on the central heap while calling out card numbers in the correct ascending order from Ace to King to Ace to King.

The cheating is inevitable because the players *must* say 'Two', 'Three', 'Four', or whatever number happens to be next in sequence, whether or not they actually happen to be playing the card whose number they're calling. Of course, any player who thinks that another player may be saying one thing while playing another can call out 'Cheat!' When this happens, the challenged player must turn up the card he has just played and if it turns out that he was cheating, as a penalty he must accept one card from each of the other players. However if the challenged player was not cheating, he is allowed to give one of his cards to the player who challenged him.

The first player to get rid of all his cards is the winner.

Fish
Card-game for two or more

Grandmothers have been teaching their grandchildren this elegant little card-game since the end of the eighteenth century. Playing Fish is rather like playing Happy Families, but this game has more class.

Deal five cards to each player and place the remainder face downwards in the centre of the table. The player to the left of the dealer starts the ball rolling by asking any other player for a particular card. He can only ask for that card if he already has one of the same value in his hand. If the player asked has the card, then he must hand it over, and the player who did the asking gets another chance to ask another player (or the same player) for another card.

However, if the player he has asked does not have the asked-for card, he gets the reply 'Fish!' and has to fish the top card off the pile of cards sitting in the middle of the table. It then becomes the turn of the player who said 'Fish!'

Whenever a player has collected four cards of equal value, he places them face upwards on the table in front of him. The first player to get rid of all his cards is the winner, but if two or more players go out together, the one with the most sets of four is the overall winner.

Mexican Rummy
Card-game for three, four or five

The charm of this game is that it involves that neglected playing card the Joker. Not only that, it calls for *two* full packs plus Jokers. The aim of the game is to get rid of all your cards, and you start with ten of them. When ten cards have been dealt to all the players, the next card that is turned up is placed by the stock pile and forms the base of the discard pile.

The player to the left of the dealer begins and he starts by taking a card from either the discard pile (which is face up) or from the stock pile (which is face down). He can then lay down three or more cards of the same denomination if he has them or a suit-sequence of three or more cards (with the Aces counting as either high or low). If he can't lay down any kind of combination he must discard one card and it becomes the next player's turn. Once a player has laid at least one combination on the table, when it is his turn he can add cards to any of the combinations already on the table. A Joker can count as any card and, if laid down in a sequence at the open end, may be moved to the other end and replaced by the correct normal card. Each Joker, however, can only be moved once in the game.

As soon as one of the players is out, the game is over, and the player who went out is the winner and receives points (or pounds) from the other players to the value of the cards remaining in their hands, with Jokers counting as fifteen, Aces as eleven, court cards as ten, and the rest as their face value.

Oh hell!
Card-game for three or more

This game goes on for thirteen full rounds, so pack sandwiches and a flask of cocoa before you start. In Round One, seven cards are dealt to each player and the remaining cards are cut to discover Trumps (that is to say, whatever happens to be the suit of the card that is revealed when the pack is cut will make all the other cards of that suit played during that round more powerful than any of the cards in the other three suits). Starting to the left of the dealer, players must announce how many 'tricks' they are going to make. (When each player plays a card, following the suit of the first card played if at all possible, the player who plays the highest card of that particular suit or — not having any cards of that suit — the highest card in the suit that is Trumps, wins all the cards played and takes the trick.) Play then begins and the object of the exercise is to make the number of tricks you forecast, no more and no less. The player to the left of the dealer plays the first card, the others follow suit, or being unable to follow suit, either play a Trump card or a throw-away card from one of the other two suits. The player who wins the trick, plays the next card. When all seven hands have been played, Round One is over and the score is totted up. Players who forecast that they would win no tricks and have won none, score 10 points. Players who forecast winning one trick, score 11, for two tricks 12, for three 13, for four 14, and so on. Players who failed to do as they forecast, either by winning tricks when they said they wouldn't or by winning the wrong number of tricks, score nothing.

In Round Two, six cards are dealt to each player and the whole process is repeated. In Round Three, five cards; in Round Four, four cards; in Round Five, three cards; in Round Six, two cards; in Round Seven, one card; in Round Eight, two cards; in Round Nine, three cards; in Round Ten, four cards; in Round Eleven, five cards; in Round Twelve, six cards; and in Round Thirteen, seven cards.

At the end of all thirteen rounds, the player with the highest score is the winner.

Old Maid
Card-game for two or more

Remove the friendly Queen of Hearts from an ordinary pack of cards and deal out the remaining fifty-one cards as equally as possible. The players then sort through their hands and place on the table any pairs they happen to have. If a player has three cards that match, he can still only put down two of them. However, if he has all four, he can place them on the table as two pairs.

Once the pairs have been sorted out, the player to the left of the dealer begins by holding out his cards, fanned out but face downwards, to the player on his left who chooses one of the cards and takes it. If that card gives that player a pair, he must place the pair on the table. If it doesn't, he simply retains the card. Either way, it's now his turn to fan out his cards and offer them to the player on his left who picks one and repeats the process.

This carries on until all the cards have been paired off when one unfortunate player will be left holding one of the Queens. That player is the Old Maid and loses the game.

Pelmanism
Card-game for two or more

Named, not surprisingly, after the Pelman Institute, where the game was created as a memory-testing device, Pelmanism can be played by any number of people with any number of packs of cards. To begin, lay out all fifty-two (or 104, or 156 or 208 or however many) cards on a large table, face downwards and at random. In his turn, each player can now turn up two cards — any two cards — and if those two cards happen to form a pair he wins them, takes them from the table and has an extra turn. If they don't form a pair, having studied them and made sure that everyone else has had a chance to see them he replaces them face downwards and it becomes the turn of the next player.

Once all the cards have been paired off and claimed by the players, the individual with the most cards is the winner.

Slobberhannes
Card-game for four

Its unfortunate name puts a lot of people off this remarkably good German card-game. You play it with a pack from which all the cards below Seven have been withdrawn, so that it's Aces high and Sevens low. The dealer begins by giving each player one card at a time face downwards. Once the cards have been dealt, play commences and the aim of the game is to avoid winning the first trick, the last trick or any trick that includes the Queen of Clubs. There are no trumps and you must follow suit if you can. If you win one of the fatal tricks you lose one point; if you win two you lose two; if you win all three, you lose four points. At the end of a set number of hands, the player with least points has won.

Here are ten essential card-tricks. Once you have mastered the tricks themselves, you can build them into a more elaborate entertainment with a little bit of showmanship. The more flair you show, the more fun you will give your audience. One requires an element of sleight-of-hand, two require some preparation, two require an accomplice and all call for a little practice and as much theatrical enthusiasm as you can muster. They may seem simple to you, but you'll be surprised how they can fool your audience if really well presented.

All-purpose trick

The effect: You invite any member of the audience to select any card from a full pack, look at it and replace it on top of the pack, cut the cards and return the cards to you. You now ask them to concentrate on the card of their choice and you tell them what it is.

The explanation: When shuffling the pack, before passing it to the member of the audience, you make a mental note of the *bottom* card, so that when he has placed the card of his choice on top of the pack and cut the cards, his card will be below the card you've memorised. When he returns the cards to you, you flash through them quickly and announce the identity of the chosen card.

Counting the pips trick

The effect: You explain to your audience that, for the purposes of the trick, each card is worth the value of its 'pips' (meaning that the Ace will count as one, the five as five, the nine as nine) and that the court cards (Knave, Queen, King) are worth ten. You then invite a member of the audience to select any six cards from a full pack and to place them face downwards on the table. Now leave the room and get him, while you're out, to place on top of each of the six cards as many cards as necessary to make the total number of 'pips' plus the number of additional cards come to twelve. (For example, on a Two, he'd put ten cards, on a Five seven, on a Queen two, and so on). When he has done this you return to the room, take the remaining cards from him and tell him exactly what the pips add up to on the bottom six cards.

The explanation: When you return to the room, simply take the remaining cards from the member of the audience, count them and add the number 26. Believe it or not, this will give you the total number of pips on the bottom cards. Should there not be enough cards left to complete the six heaps, ask the member of the audience how many cards he is short of, subtract this from 25, and again you will come up with the right answer.

Court cards trick

The effect: You take an ordinary pack of playing-cards and sort out all the Kings, Queens and Knaves. These you put together in any part of the pack. You now invite a member of the audience to cut the pack a dozen times — and tell him that thanks to your magic powers, none of the court cards will be disturbed.

The explanation: You don't have to do a thing: simply trust your luck. The odds are 500 to 1 in your favour that even after the pack has been cut twelve times, the Kings, Queens and Knaves will still be all together!

Eccentrick

The effect: You give a member of the audience a pack of cards, invite him to shuffle them and select any card he chooses. Then ask him to place the remaining cards on the table and cut them into two packs. Ask him now to place the card he chose on top of one of the packs and when he has done so tell him to place the other cards on top and straighten the whole pack. This done you tap the side of the cards with your magic wand (or a pencil) and, lo and behold, they separate at the very point where the chosen card is located!

The explanation: You have concealed between the finger and thumb of your right hand a few tiny grains of dry salt. When you tell him on which pack to place his card, you indicate it by touching it and as you do so the few grains of salt will fall on to the cards. He then covers the salt with his card and covers his card with all the other cards. When you tap the side of the cards you will find that they separate at the point where you placed the salt.

Futuristrick

The effect: You hand a pack of cards to a member of the audience and invite him to shuffle them. Now tell him to choose a colour, either black or red. Having chosen his colour, you invite him to select two cards at a time from the pack. He can look at each pair and if they both happen to be of the colour of his choice, he keeps them: if both are the same colour, which is *not* the colour of his choice, he gives them to you: if they are of different colours, he discards them. Before he begins to select his pairs of cards, simply tell him that by the time he has finished you (or he, as the case may be) will have four extra cards. When he counts up at the end of the trick, he will find that you were absolutely right.

The explanation: Before handing him the pack, remove four cards, either four black cards or four red cards. If you have removed four black cards, the end-result will be a surplus of four red cards, so that if he has chosen black, you are the one who will end up with four more cards, but if he has chosen red, then he will get the four extra cards.

Mind-reading trick

The effect: You ask a member of the audience to shuffle the pack, select five cards without looking at them and lay them face-down on the table. You now leave the room and invite another member of the audience to look at one of the cards while you're out, memorising both the card and its position, say, from left to right, numbering them first, second, third, fourth and fifth. You now return to the room, collect up the cards, put them in your pocket for a moment, enquire the exact position of the chosen card, return the five cards to the member of the audience, invite him to shuffle them and lay them face upwards on the table. You now tell him which card he chose.

The explanation: Before starting the trick, you have removed and memorised four cards and placed them in your pocket. When collecting the five cards from the table you pick them up in the correct order and are careful when putting them in your pocket not to muddle them up with the four cards already planted there. Having found out in which position the chosen card lies, you remove it from the quintet and join it to the four planted cards which you now produce from your pocket and hand over to the member of the audience. He shuffles and reveals them and you tell him that his card is whichever one wasn't part of the planted four.

Nine-card trick

The effect: You lay out nine cards on the table, leave the room, and while you are out invite the audience to choose one of the nine cards. You return and a member of the audience points to each card in turn asking you if this is the card the audience has chosen. When he has touched all the cards, you pick up the right card.

The explanation: The member of the audience who points to the cards is a confederate. He will touch each card in a particular place and the place he touches will indicate the card's position in the layout. So, if the confederate touches all the cards in the top right-hand corner, you know the card you want is located in the top right-hand corner of the lay-out, and if he touches each card right in the middle you know the card you want is the central one.

Odds and Evens trick

The effect: You give a complete pack of cards to a member of the audience and invite him to cut them, and place one half of the pack in your right hand, the other in your left. You then tell him whether you are holding an odd number of cards in each hand or an even number.

The explanation: Before passing the pack to the member of the audience, you have arranged the cards so that there is one red, one black, one red, one black, and so on, right through the pack. When he has cut the pack and given the two parts back to you, simply glance at the bottom cards. If both are black or both are red, each part contains an even number of cards. If one is black and the other red, the number in each pack are uneven.

Picture trick

The effect: You hold up a pack of cards, so that you cannot see the front card but the audience can. You close your eyes and tell the audience that by simply feeling the cards you can tell whether or not they are court cards. You proceed to show them a whole series of cards, eyes closed or blindfolded all the while, telling them whenever a court card turns up.

The explanation: A confederate is involved. He must be sitting near you, so that whenever a court card appears, he can press your foot gently with his.

Telepatrick

The effect: Deal out three heaps containing seven cards each, all of them face-upwards. Now invite a member of the audience to think of any card he likes and tell you which of the three heaps it's in. Gather the heaps together and repeat the process. Repeat it once more. Then sort through the cards and reveal to an astonished public the card the member of the audience has chosen.

The explanation: First time round, whichever heap the member of the audience says his card is in is the heap you put between the other two heaps when you gather the cards together. When you deal them out for the second time, you put the first card on the left, the second in the middle, the third on the right, the fourth on the left and so on. You again ask which heap contains the chosen card and again put that heap between the other two. You deal them out for the third time just as before, and again as before invite the member of the audience to tell you in which heap his card may be found. Put that heap between the other two, turn the cards over, so that they are face downwards, and count out eleven cards. The chosen card will be the eleventh card.

Card castles

If patience and card-games and tricks don't entertain you, there is still something you can do with your cards. You can build castles and palaces with them. You need a completely flat surface, preferably covered with felt or baize, and as many cards as you can find. Though more expensive and less durable, linen cards are better for castle building than plastic ones. You take the cards and lean them up one against the other, balancing them as best you can and eventually building one layer on top of another.

If you are very clever you will build a card castle with fourteen storeys, with eight cards making up each storey — and once you've managed that you can write off to the *Guinness Book of Records* because you will have equalled the latest card-castle world record.

4. PUZZLE PAGES

There are over fifty different puzzles in this chapter and, while you can enjoy trying to solve them on your own, they have been specially chosen because they are all suitable for 'group solution'. Coins, matches, pencils and your wits are all you need to have about you.

Coins
Solutions on page 65

1. Take a dozen coins and arrange them in a square like this, so that you can count four coins along each side:

   O   O   O   O
   O   O
   O   O
   O   O   O   O

   Now use exactly the same coins to form another square so that you can count five coins along each side.

2. Arrange six coins in the form of a cross like this:

Now move just one of them to create two rows with four coins in each row.

3. Arrange ten coins in a pyramid like this:

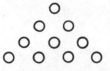

Now move just three of them and turn the pyramid upside down.

4. Lay three 1p and three 2p pieces in a row like this:

Now in just three moves, *moving two adjacent coins at a time,* you must end up with a row of coins where the 2p and the 1p pieces alternate. And when you have finished there mustn't be any gaps between coins.

5. Lay four 1p and four 2p pieces in a row like this:

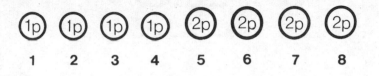

Now in just four moves, again moving two adjacent coins at a time, you must end up with a row in which there are no gaps and the 2p and 1p pieces alternate.

6. Arrange seven coins in a pattern like this and you will find you have five rows with three coins in each row:

Now add an extra two coins to the existing pattern so as to have ten rows with three coins in each row.

7. Take a dozen coins and arrange them in a particular pattern so that you have three straight lines with an odd number of coins in each line.

Matches
Solutions on page 66

For the first six puzzles you have to start with a grid made up of twenty-four matches and looking like this:

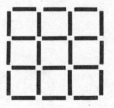

1. Remove four matches and leave five squares.
2. Remove six matches and leave five squares.
3. Remove six matches and leave three squares.
4. Remove eight matches and leave four squares.
5. Remove eight matches and leave three squares.
6. Remove eight matches and leave two squares.

7. Now here's an equation with Roman numerals that doesn't make sense:

$$IV - II = V$$

Move just one match to make the equation valid.

8. Using twenty-four matches construct six squares.

9. Using the same twenty-four matches make 110 squares.

10. Here are twelve matches forming six equilateral triangles:

Move four matches and leave three equilateral triangles.

11. Here are six matches:

Add five more and make nine.

12. Remove four matches and leave four triangles:

13. Using eleven matches, construct the outline of a Greek temple like this:

First move two matches and make eleven squares. Then move four matches and make fifteen squares.

14. And here's a subtle one to end with. Using eight matches and Roman numerals, prove that half of twelve is seven.

Figures and numbers
Solutions on page 69

1. Humbert Humbert is 40. Lolita is 13. How many years ago was Humbert Humbert four times as old as Lolita?

2. Find a number whose double exceeds its half by 99.

3. Which number is the odd one out: 14, 28, 84, 49, 140, 65, 35, 21?

4. Find a number which is increased by one fifth of its value if the order of its digits is reversed.

5. A man drives a certain distance at 60 mph and arrives one hour earlier than if he had driven at 50 mph. What was the distance?

6. What is the smallest number that when divided by 2, 3, 4, 5, 6, 7, 8, 9 and 10 respectively will leave remainders of 1, 2, 3, 4, 5, 6, 7, 8 and 9?

7. Here's a lunatic question: if a quarter of forty is six, what's a third of twenty?

8. What's the difference between six dozen dozen and a half dozen dozen?

9. Take the digits 1, 2, 3, 4, 5, 6, 7, 8, 9 and 0 and arrange them in the form of a simple sum that will add up to 100.

10. Anton Chekhov loved letter-writing (his published letters extend to eighteen volumes), but whenever he wrote a letter he used two sheets of paper and for every twelve letters he wrote he threw away one sheet of paper. How many letters could he have written with only 100 sheets of paper?

11. What are the next two numbers in this series: 1, 4, 9, 16, 25, 36, —, —?

12. Chris Brasher once ran a mile in 4.12 minutes. Dave Bedford once ran 4.12 miles in one hour. Which of the two was the faster runner?

Words and letters
Solutions on page 69

1. In this series what are the four missing letters — and why?

   H A P O T R
   H A P O T
   T T W T M G
   — — — —

2. Think of a word that contains just one vowel and contains that vowel six times.

3. Find the missing letter: Z V A — B W C

4. Insert just one letter of the alphabet as many times as necessary amid this series of letters and you'll get an intelligible phrase.

   What is it?

   ALHOUGHHEWOOSIERED
   HEYOLDHEOFOLDALE

5. An atlas might help you with this puzzle. Which is the odd man out:

   a LAYTI
   b NOPLAD
   c SOAKVACCHOZILE
   d FECARN
   e LAIBUGAR

6. With these two sets of five letters find the last letter in the second set:
   HORSE   IPST—

7. Think of a word that's an anagram of that well-known Mexican delicacy: ROAST MULES.

8. What word, beginning with an H and ending with an N, contains six other words within its spelling — and to find those words you don't need to transpose a single letter.

9. Fit two commas, two semi-colons, one question mark and one full stop in amongst the following words and construct a logical sentence:
   That that is is that that is not is not is not that it it is

10. In order to create two different everyday words out of the five letters Y, T, C, E and H, you need a sixth letter. What's the letter and what are the two words?

11. Think of two English words that contain the five vowels A-E-I-O-U once and once only in their alphabetical order.

12. Why is this unlucky: TTTTIIEEYEARDNFRHHH

13. And here's a puzzle with a Shakespearian flavour. Which one of the following three series of letters is the odd man out — and why:

    a KGKIGNON   *b* KRNLAGEI   *c* KNHIONGJ

14. Think of an everyday English word that contains nine letters but only one vowel.

Dots
Solutions on page 70

1. Without taking your pencil from the page and without going over the same line twice, join the nine dots with four straight lines:

2. Without taking your pencil from the page and without going over the same line twice, join the sixteen dots with six straight lines:

```
.   .   .   .
.   .   .   .
.   .   .   .
.   .   .   .
```

3. Without taking your pencil from the page and without going over the same line twice, join the twenty-five dots with eight straight lines:

```
.   .   .   .   .
.   .   .   .   .
.   .   .   .   .
.   .   .   .   .
.   .   .   .   .
```

Coins—solutions

1.

2.

3. Move the top coin below the bottom row; then move the two end coins from the bottom row to the ends of row 2.

4. Move coins 1 and 2 to the right of 6; move coins 6 and 1 to the right of 2; move coins 3 and 4 to the right of 5.

5. Move coins 6 and 7 to the left of 1; move coins 3 and 4 to the right of 5; move coins 7 and 1 to the right of 2; move coins 4 and 8 to the right of 6.

6.

7.

Matches—solutions

1.

2.

3.

4.

5.

6.

7. IV + I = V

8.

9.

10.

11. N I N E

12.

13.

14.

$$XII \longrightarrow VII$$

Figures and numbers—solutions

1. 4
2. 66
3. 65 — all the other numbers are divisible by 7
4. 45
5. 300 miles
6. 2519
7. 4
8. 792
9. $50\frac{1}{2} + 49\frac{38}{76} = 100$
10. 48
11. 49, 64
12. Chris Brasher

Words and letters—solutions

1. P G T W. The letters are the initials of the first four lines of that evergreen ditty 'Pop Goes the Weasel'.
2. Indivisibility.
3. X.
4. T. Although the two tots tittered they told the oft told tale.
5. The letters are anagrams of the names of countries: Italy, Poland, Czechoslovakia, France, Bulgaria. Czechoslovakia is the odd one out because it's land-locked.
6. F.
7. SOMERSAULT.

8. HEREIN: here, her, he, ere, rein, in.
9. That that is, is; that that is not, is not; is not that it? It is.
10. S. SCYTHE and CHESTY.
11. Facetious and abstemious.
12. The letters spell FRIDAY THE THIRTEENTH.
13. *a* is an anagram of KING KONG, *b* is an anagram of KING LEAR and *c* is an anagram of KING JOHN, which makes *a* the odd man out as Shakespeare never wrote a play about King Kong.
14. Strengths.

Dots—solutions

Start at S and follow the arrows.

1.

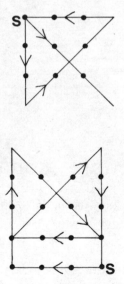

2.

3.

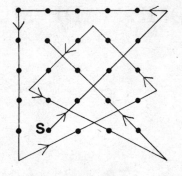

5. HOME-MADE MUSIC

Not much more than half a century ago the promise of 'an evening at the phonograph' would have seemed most enticing. Today the idea seems tame. We are so used to having music wherever we go — in the car, in the shops, in the bath — that to settle down to listen to the phonograph, or its latter day equivalents, the record-player and tape recorder, for a whole evening would seem absurd. Of course, stereo buffs do it regularly, but in the age of universal Muzak a home-made record and cassette concert is hardly considered the ultimate in swinging home entertainment.

As it happens, once in a while, and providing the domestic concert doesn't last too long, a couple of hours seated round the gramophone or the recorder listening to records and tapes can prove quite a novelty — especially when the pieces played have been chosen to suit the audience's taste and the mood of the moment. All the same, however well organised these little electronic concerts are, they are very unlikely to become regular events.

Novelty is what we crave for nowadays and, as far as music is concerned, the way to achieve it is to return in spirit to the heyday of our great-grandparents, when people had no alternative but to make their own music, and did so with great charm.

The Victorians were particularly adept at coming up with home-made instruments. You can make music (of sorts) by banging trays or pots and pans with wooden spoons, by filling a row of bottles with varying amounts of water and striking the bottles with a knife, by taking soup spoons and playing them against your knees like castanets, by covering the teeth of a comb with tissue paper and blowing on it and by filling saucer-shaped champagne glasses with water and rubbing their rims with your forefinger.

The last device sounds the least likely, yet makes the sweetest noise. It enjoyed an enormous vogue in London in the 1760s and is about due for a comeback. All you do is set out a row of champagne glasses and fill each one with a different amount of water. Naturally, the note you get depends on the amount of water in the glass: with more water you get a higher note, with less, a lower one, Having filled the glasses, you should wet the rims of the glasses and dampen your forefinger. Now all you need to do is pass your forefinger lightly but firmly around the rim and a note will sound. Yes, it does seem improbable, but before you reject the idea without trying it, remember that both Mozart and Gluck composed music for such glasses.

Of course, much as Mozart and Gluck loved musical glasses, it has to be admitted they preferred the human voice. And our great-grandparents, while enjoying their home-made instruments, were never so happy as when making their music without any kind of mechanical aid. There were some eccentrics who took the notion of self-made music to extremes and blew raspberries or broke wind as a form of entertainment, but they were exceptional — and still would be. Someone who would also be regarded as unusual today, but whose activities would have seemed commonplace a century ago, is the whistler.

Just as people do still imitate train sounds to amuse their friends and catch the eye of television producers, so do people still imitate bird song by whistling. The Victorian and Edwardian whistler, however, would never be content to simply sound like the 10.15 to Doncaster or the mating call of a chaffinch. When he whistled, he whistled a proper tune, accompanied at the very least on the piano, and went on for quite a while.

There is an art to whistling and it's one that can only be mastered by those who have the basic knack and who are prepared to put in the long hours of practice that are quite essential. The world's greatest siffleur — as high-class whistlers are known — was Charles Capper and, while he never revealed the secrets of his art, he did offer drawing-room whistlers two sound pieces of advice: 'The first is never to laugh when performing. The veriest novice knows that his risibilities must be well under control before he can whistle a single note, so that it is essential for him — no matter what funny incident is noticed and appeals to him — to hold tight to his gravity. The second is that lip-salves should be strictly avoided, as they render the lips susceptible to cracks and cold; besides, they make a film which sticks and prevents clear whistling.'

Naturally, the form of music-making that gave most pleasure to the performers and their audiences was singing at the piano. The numbers that follow are classics of their kind and come from Michael Turner's magical volume, *The Parlour Song Book: a Casquet of Vocal Gems*, published by Michael Joseph, by whose permission they are reproduced. They have been sung by home entertainers for generations, so never mind how poorly your accompanist plays the piano, never mind how croaky you sound, simply sing these numbers — with your friends joining in the choruses — and you'll discover what home-made music is all about.

Come into the garden, Maud

Written by Alfred, Lord Tennyson; composed by M. W. Balfe.

Come in - to the gar - den,

Maud, For the black bat, Night, is flown;

Come in - to the gar - den, Maud, I am here at the gate a -

- lone. I am here,__ at the gate a - lone. And the

wood - bine spi - ces are waft - ed a - broad, And the musk of the ro - ses

blown, For a breeze of morn - ing moves,__ And the

plan - et of love is on high, Be - gin - ning to faint in the

light that she loves, On a bed of daf - fo - dil sky, To

-lone,   I   am   here ——————— at the   gate   a -

- lone!

Queen   Rose   of   the   rose - bud,

Gar - den of girls,   Come hi -ther,   the dan - ces   are   done;   In

gloss   of sa - tin   and glim - mer   of pearls, Queen   li - ly   and rose,   in

one.___ Shine out lit-tle head sun-ning o-ver with curls To the

flow-ers and be___ their Sun. Shine out! Shine out! and be their Sun.

Come in-to the gar - den, Maud, For the black bat, Night, is

flown; Come in-to the gar - den Maud. She is

com-ing, my own, my sweet, Were it e-ver so ai-ry a

Home! Sweet home!

Written by John Howard Payne; composed by Sir Henry Bishop.

1. 'Mid pleas - ures and Pà - la - ces though___ we may roam,___ Be it

e - ver so hum - ble there's no___ place like home!___ A

charm___ from_ the skies seems to hal - low us there,___ Which

seek___through the world, is ne'er met with else - where.

Home! Home,___ sweet sweet Home! There's no___place like

Largo *tr* **Tempo Imo**

Home!___ There's no___ place like Home!___

colla voce *pp* *ff* *ten.*

più animato

2. An Ex - ile from Home, Splen-dour

daz – zles in vain!_____ Oh! give_____ me my low – ly thatch'd

Cot-tage a – gain!_____ The Birds_____ sing-ing gai-ly that

came_____ at my call,_____ Give me them_____ with the peace of mind_____

dear-er_____ than all! Home! Home,_____ sweet sweet_____

Home! There's no_____ place like Home!_____ There's no_____place like Home!_____

I'll take you home again, Kathleen

Written and composed by Thomas P. Westendorf.

1. I'll take you home a-gain, Kath-leen, A-cross the o-cean wild and wide, To where your heart has ev-er been, Since first you were my bon-ny bride. The ro-ses all have left your

Jeanie with the light-brown hair

Written and composed by Stephen C. Foster.

Allegretto moderato

I dream of Jea-nie with the light-brown hair, Borne like a va-pour

on the sum-mer air; I see her trip-ping where the bright streams play,

Hap - py as the dai - sies that dance on her way; Ma-ny were the wild notes her

mer-ry voice would pour, Ma-ny were the blithe birds that war - bled them o'er.

CHORUS

Oh!___ I dream of Jea - nie with the light brown hair,

I dream of Jea - nie with the light brown hair,

I dream of Jea - nie with the light brown hair,

Float-ing like a va-pour on the soft sum-mer air.

Float-ing like a va-pour on the soft sum-mer air.

Float-ing like a va-pour on the soft sum-mer air.

p

Love's old sweet song

Written by J. Clifton Bingham; composed by James L. Molloy.

Once in the dear dead days be-yond re-call, When on the world the

mists be-gan to fall, Out of the dreams that rose in hap-py throng,

Low to our hearts Love sung an old sweet song; And in the dusk where

fell the fire-light gleam, Soft - ly it - self in - to our dream.

rit.

CHORUS
p a tempo

Just a song at twi - light, when the lights are low,

p

And the flick' - ring sha-dows soft - ly come and go, Tho' the heart be

f

mf

wea - ry, sad the day and long, Still to us at twi - light

rit.

comes Love's old song, Comes Love's old sweet___ song.

f rit.

sempre Ped.

O for the wings of a dove

*Written by William Bartholomew; composed by Felix
    Mendelssohn Bartholdy.*

The yellow rose of Texas

Written and composed by J. K.

There's a yel-low rose in Tex-as That I am going to see, No

o - ther dar - key knows her, No dar - key on - ly me; She

cried so when I left her. It like to broke my heart, And

if I ev - er find_ her, We nev - er-more will part.

CHORUS

She's the sweet-est rose of co-lour This dar-key ev - er knew, Her

She's the sweet-est rose of co-lour This dar-key ev - er knew, Her

She's the sweet - est rose of co-lour This dar-key ev - er knew, Her

p staccato

eyes are bright as dia-monds, They spar - kle like the dew; You may

eyes are bright as dia-monds, They spar - kle like the dew; You may

eyes are bright as dia-monds, They spar - kle like the dew; You may

And for this medley of even more familiar classics from the parlour repertory, who needs music?

The animals went in two by two

The animals went in two by two,
Hurrah! Hurrah!
The animals went in two by two,
Hurrah! Hurrah!
The animals went in two by two,
The elephant and the kangaroo,
And they all went into the ark
For to get out of the rain.

The animals went in three by
  three,
Hurrah! Hurrah!
The animals went in three by
  three,
Hurrah! Hurrah!
The animals went in three by
  three,
The wasp, the ant and the
  bumble-bee,
And they all . . .

The animals went in four by four,
Hurrah! Hurrah!
The animals went in four by four,
Hurrah! Hurrah!
The animals went in four by four,
The great hippopotamus stuck in
  the door,
And they all . . .

The animals went in five by five,
Hurrah! Hurrah!
The animals went in five by five,
Hurrah! Hurrah!
The animals went in five by five,
By eating each other they kept
  alive,
And they all . . .

The animals went in six by six,
Hurrah! Hurrah!
The animals went in six by six,
Hurrah! Hurrah!
The animals went in six by six,
They turned out the monkey
  because of his tricks,
And they all . . .

The animals went in seven by
  seven,
Hurrah! Hurrah!
The animals went in seven by
  seven,
Hurrah! Hurrah!
The animals went in seven by
  seven,
The little pig thought he was
  going to heaven,
And they all . . .

Auld lang syne

Should auld acquaintance be
   forgot,
   And never brought to min'?
Should auld acquaintance be
   forgot,
   And auld lang syne?

For auld lang syne, my dear,
   For auld lang syne,
We'll tak' a cup o' kindness yet
For auld lang syne.

And surely ye'll be your pint-
   stowp,
   And surely I'll be mine!
And we'll tak' a cup o' kindness
   yet,
   For auld lang syne.

For auld lang syne . . .

We twa ha'e run about the braes,
   And pou'd the gowans fine;

But we've wandered mony a weary
   foot
   Sin' auld lang syne.

For auld lang syne . . .

We twa ha'e paidl't i' the burn,
   Frae mornin' sun till dine;
But seas between us braid ha'e
   roared
   Sin' auld lang syne.

For auld lang syne . . .

And there's a hand, my trusty
   fiere,
   And gie's a hand o' thine!
And we'll tak' a right guid willie-
   waught,
   For auld lang syne.

For auld lang syne . . .

Boney was a warrior

Boney was a warrior,
Way-ay-yah!
Boney was a warrior,
John France-wah!

Boney beat the Rooshians,
Way-ay-yah! . . .

Boney beat the Prooshians,
Way-ay-yah! . . .

Boney went to Mossycow,
Way-ay-yah! . . .

Boney he came back again,
Way-ay-yah! . . .

Boney went to El-be-ah,
Way-ay-yah! . . .

Boney went to Waterloo,
Way-ay-yah! . . .

Boney he was sent away,
Way-ay-yah! . . .

Boney broke his heart and died,
Way-ay-yah! . . .

Boney was a warrior.
Way-ay-yah! . . .

Camptown races

The Camptown ladies sing this song,
Doodah! Doodah!
The Camptown race-track five miles long,
Oh! Doodah day!
I come down there wid my hat caved in,
Doodah! Doodah!
I go back home wid a pocket full of tin,
Oh! Doodah day!
Gwine to run all night!
Gwine to run all day!
I'll bet my money on the bob-tail nag,
Somebody bet on the bay.

The long-tail filly and the big black hoss,
Doodah! Doodah!
They fly the track an' they both cut across,
Oh! Doodah day!
The blind hoss sticking in a big mud hole,
Doodah! Doodah!
Can't touch the bottom wid a ten-foot pole,
Oh! Doodah day . . .

Old muley cow come on the track,
The bob-tail fling her over his back,
Then fly along like a railroad car,
And run a race wid a shootin' star,
Oh! Doodah day . . .

Oh, see them flyin' on a ten-mile heat,
Around the race-track then repeat,
I win my money on the bob-tail nag,
I keep my money in an old tow bag,
Oh! Doodah day . . .

Charlie is my darling

Charlie is m'darling, m'darling, m'darling,
Charlie is m'darling, the young Chevalier.

'Twas on a Monday morning,
Right early in the year,
When Charlie came to our town,
The young Chevalier,
Oh! Charlie is m'darling, m'darling, m'darling . . .

As he came marching up the street,
The pipes played loud and clear,
And all the folks came running out,
To meet the Chevalier,
Oh! Charlie . . .

Wi' Hieland bonnets on their heads,
And claymores bright and clear,
They came to fight for Scotland's right,
And for the Chevalier,
Oh! Charlie . . .

They've left their bonnie Hieland hills,
Their wives and children dear,
To draw the sword for Scotland's Lord,
The young Chevalier.
Oh! Charlie . . .

The grand old Duke of York

Oh, the grand old Duke of York,
He had ten thousand men.
He marched them up to the top of the hill
And he marched them down again.

And when they were up they were up,
And when they were down they were down,
And when they were only half way up
They were neither up nor down.

Oh, the grand old Duke of York . . .

They look'd all a-round and a-round,
But nothing at all could they find,
Except a big hay-stack in a field,
And that they left behind.

Oh, the grand old Duke of York . . .

The Englishman said, 'Tis a stack',
The Scotsman — he said, 'Nay',
The Irishman said it was a church
With the steeple blown away.

Oh, the grand old Duke of York . . .

John Brown's body

John Brown's body lies a-mould'ring in the grave,
John Brown's body lies a-mould'ring in the grave,
John Brown's body lies a-mould'ring in the grave,
His soul is marching on!

Glory, Glory, Hallelujah!
Glory, Glory, Hallelujah!
Glory, Glory, Hallelujah!
His soul is marching on!

The stars in heaven now are looking kindly down,
The stars in heaven now are looking kindly down,
The stars in heaven now are looking kindly down,
On the grave of old John Brown.

Glory, Glory, . . .

He's gone to be a soldier in the army of the Lord,
He's gone to be a soldier in the army of the Lord,
He's gone to be a soldier in the army of the Lord,
His soul is marching on.

Glory, Glory . . .

The Lincolnshire poacher

When I was bound apprentice, in famous Lincolnshire,
Full well I served my master for more than seven year,
Till I took up to poaching, as you shall quickly hear;
Oh! 'tis my delight on a shining night in the season of the year.
Oh! 'tis my delight on a shining night in the season of the year.

As me and my companions were setting of a snare,
'Twas then we spied the gamekeeper, for him we did not care,
For we can wrestle and fight, my boys, and jump o'er anywhere;
Oh! 'tis my delight . . .

As me and my companions were setting four or five,
And taking on 'em up again, we caught a hare alive,
We took the hare alive, my boys, and through the woods did steer;
Oh! 'tis my delight . . .

I took him on my shoulder, and then we trudged home,
We took him to a neighbour's house and sold him for a crown,
We sold him for a crown, my boys, I did not tell you where;
Oh! 'tis my delight . . .

Success to every gentleman who lives in Lincolnshire,
Success to every poacher who wants to sell a hare,
Bad luck to every gamekeeper who will not sell his deer;
Oh! 'tis my delight . . .

Loch Lomond

By yon bonnie banks, and by yon bonnie braes
Where the sun shines bright on Loch Lomond,
Where me and my true love were ever wont to gae,
On the bonnie bonnie banks o' Loch Lomond.

Oh, ye'll tak' the high road and I'll tak' the low road,
And I'll be in Scotland a-fore ye;
But me and my true love we'll never meet again
On the bonnie, bonnie banks o' Loch Lomond.

'Twas there that we parted in yon shady glen
On the steep, steep side o' Ben Lomond,
Where in purple hue many Hieland hills we'd view,
And the moon coming out in the gloaming.

Oh, ye'll tak' the high road and I'll tak' the low road . . .

Men of Harlech

Hark! I hear the foe advancing,
Barbed steeds are proudly
    prancing,
Helmets, in the sunbeams
    glancing,
Glitter through the trees.
Men of Harlech, lie ye dreaming?
See ye not their falchions
    gleaming?
While their pennants gaily
    streaming
Flutter in the breeze.
From the rocks rebounding,
Let the war-cry sounding
Summon all
At Cambria's call,
The haughty foe surrounding.
Men of Harlech, on to glory!
See, your banner famed in story,
Waves these burning words
    before ye,
'Britain scorns to yield'.

Mid the fray, see dead and dying,
Friends and foe together lying,
All around the arrows flying,
Scatter sudden death.
Frightened steeds are wildly
    neighing,
Brazen trumpets hoarsely
    braying,
Wounded men for mercy praying
With their parting breath.
See they're in disorder!
Comrades, keep close order!
Ever they
Shall rue the day
They ventured o'er the border.
Now the Saxon flees before us,
Vict'ry's banner floateth o'er us,
Raise the loud exulting chorus,
'Britain wins the field'.

Michael Finnigin

There was an old man called Michael Finnigin,
He grew whiskers on his chinigin,
The wind came up and blew them inigin,
Poor old Michael Finnigin. Beginigin.

There was an old man called Michael Finnigin,
He kicked up an awful dinigin,
Because they said he must not singigin,
Poor old Michael Finnigin. Beginigin.

There was an old man called Michael Finnigin.
He went fishing with a pinigin,
Caught a fish but dropped it inigin,
Poor old Michael Finnigin. Beginigin.

There was an old man called Michael Finnigin,
Climbed a tree and barked his shinigin,
Took off several yards of skinigin,
Poor old Michael Finnigin. Beginigin.

There was an old man called Michael Finnigin,
He grew fat and then grew thinigin,
Then he died, and had to beginigin.
Poor old Michael Finnigin. STOP.

Oh, Susanna

I came from Alabama
With my banjo on my knee.
I'm goin' to Louisiana now,
My true love for to see.
It rained all night the day I left,
The weather it was dry;
The sun so hot I froze to death;
Susanna don't you cry.

*Oh, Susanna, oh don't you cry for
   me;*
*I've come from Alabama with my
   banjo on my knee.*

I had a dream the other night,
When ev'ry thing was still,
I thought I saw Susanna dear
A-comin' down the hill.
The buck-wheat cake was in her
   mouth,
A tear was in her eye;
Says I 'I'm coming from the
   south;
Susanna, don't you cry.'

Oh, Susanna . . .

Shenandoah

Oh, Shenandoah, I long to hear
   you,
Away, you rolling river!
Oh, Shenandoah, I long to hear
   you;
Away, I'm bound to go
'Cross the wide Missouri.

Oh, Shenandoah, I love your
   daughter,
Away . . .
She sent me sailing 'cross the
   water;
Away . . .

Oh, Shenandoah, I took a notion,
Away . . .
To sail across the briny ocean;
Away . . .

Oh, Shenandoah, I long to hear
   you,
Away . . .
Oh, Shenandoah, I long to hear
   you;
Away . . .

This old man

This old man, he played one,
He played nick-nack on my drum.

Nick-nack paddy-whack,
Give a dog a bone,
This old man came rolling home.

This old man, he played two,
He played nick-nack on my shoe.

Nick-nack paddy-whack,
Give a dog a bone,
This old man came rolling home.

And so on, with the following rhymes for each number:

Three — knee
Four — door
Five — hive
Six — sticks

Seven — up in heaven
Eight — gate
Nine — line
Ten — hen

The vicar of Bray

In good King Charles's golden days,
When loyalty no harm meant,
A zealous high churchman was I,
And so I got preferment.
To teach my flock I never missed,
Kings were by God appointed,
And lost are those that dare resist,
Or touch the Lord's anointed.

And this is law I will maintain
Until my dying day,
Sir, that whatsoever King shall reign,
I'll still be the Vicar of Bray, Sir.

When royal James possessed the crown,
And Popery came in fashion,
The penal laws I hooted down,
And read the Declaration.
The Church of Rome I found would fit
Full well my constitution,
And I had been a Jesuit
But for the Revolution.

And this is law . . .

When William was our King declared
To ease the nation's grievance,
With this new wind about I steered
And swore to him allegiance.
Old principles I did revoke,
Set conscience at a distance;
Passive obedience was a joke,
A jest was non-resistance.

And this is law . . .

When royal Anne became our Queen,
The Church of England's glory,
Another face of things was seen
And I became a Tory;
Occasional conformists base,
I blamed their moderation
And thought the Church in danger was
By such prevarication.

And this is law . . .

The illustrious house of Hanover
And Protestant succession,
To them I do allegiance swear —
While they can hold possession;
For in my faith and loyalty
I never more will falter,
And George my lawful King shall be —
Until the times do alter.

And this is law . . .

Waltzing Matilda

Once a jolly swagman camped by a billabong,
Under the shade of a coolibah tree,
And he sang as he watched and waited till his billy boiled,
'You'll come a-waltzing Matilda with me!
Waltzing Matilda, waltzing Matilda,
You'll come a-waltzing Matilda with me'.
And he sang as he watched and waited till his billy boiled,
'You'll come a-waltzing Matilda with me!'

Down came a jumbuck to drink at the billabong,
Up jumped the swagman and grabbed him with glee,
And he sang as he stowed that jumbuck in his tuckerbag,
'You'll come a-waltzing Matilda with me! ...'
And he sang as he stowed that jumbuck in his tuckerbag,
'You'll come a-waltzing Matilda with me!'

Up rode the squatter, mounted on his thoroughbred,
Up rode the troopers, one, two, three;
'Whose that jolly jumbuck you've got in your tuckerbag?
You'll come a-waltzing Matilda with me! ...
Whose that jolly jumbuck you've got in your tuckerbag?
You'll come a-waltzing Matilda with me!'

Up jumped the swagman and sprang into the billabong,
'You'll never take me alive,' said he.
And his ghost may be heard as you pass by that billabong:
'You'll come a-waltzing Matilda with me! ...'
And his ghost may be heard as you pass by that billabong:
'You'll come a-waltzing Matilda with me!'

What shall we do with the drunken sailor?

What shall we do with the drunken sailor?
What shall we do with the drunken sailor?
What shall we do with the drunken sailor
Early in the morning?

Hooray and up she rises,
Hooray and up she rises,
Hooray and up she rises
Early in the morning.

Put him in the long-boat until he's sober,
Put him in the long-boat until he's sober,
Put him in the long-boat until he's sober
Early in the morning.

Hooray . . .

Pull out the plug and wet him all over,
Pull out the plug and wet him all over,
Pull out the plug and wet him all over
Early in the morning.

Hooray . . .

Put him in the scuppers with a hose-pipe on him,
Put him in the scuppers with a hose-pipe on him,
Put him in the scuppers with a hose-pipe on him
Early in the morning.

Hooray . . .

6. THE ART OF RECITATION

The art of recitation is not lost. It has been hibernating in recent years, but spring is sprung and with it the art of recitation has returned to its rightful place in the drawing-rooms and sitting-rooms and living-rooms of the land. People are rediscovering the pleasure of speaking verse and prose to their friends, and the friends are finding out that, if done well, a recitation can be a delight to listen to.

This section of verses includes several of the favourites of the Victorians and the Edwardians, as well as one or two pieces that were popular with home entertainers in the teens of this century. They are all ideal for recitation, being overtly comical or sentimental or melodramatic, and providing ample opportunity for fairly theatrical delivery, complete with dramatic gestures and (should you wish it) entertaining costumes.

It must be emphasised that if the art of recitation is not to suffer another relapse, the reciters of today must do their homework. Sight-reading out loud simply won't do. The pieces must be learnt by heart and properly prepared. The speaker must stand in a position where he can be clearly seen (and the audience must be seated comfortably or they'll get restless), he must be lit while his audience should be in darkness and he should take care — great care— to choose a recitation that will match the occasion and the mood of the audience. This selection should cater for most tastes and talents.

An awful tragedy
Neville Lynn

As I was walking late one night,
  I heard a fearful cry
Proceeding from a lonely house
  Which I was passing by.
I stood aghast; some horrid deed
  Perchance was being done.
Should I rush in heroic-like,
  Or look after Number One?
The while I paused, another groan
  Resounded on my ear —
A most blood-curdling, awful one;
  I stopped and shook with fear.
Should I make off and tell the police?
  Or should I run for good?
Or should I, could I, venture in
  To see how matters stood?
As undecided quite, I leaned
  Against a friendly wall,
I heard, O lor, another shriek,
  A struggle, and — a fall!
My hat fell off, my hair stood up
  And occupied its place;
I dropped, quite frightened, to the ground
  With white and ghastly face.
Oh, why was I born such a fool
  As to take lonely strolls?
Why had I always liked to read
  About all ghosts and ghouls?
I conjured up most awful sights:
  A woman lying dead;
Great clots of gore; a sanguined knife;
  Two ruffians, and one head!
In that short time passed through my brain
  The Horrors of Tussaud,

And ghastly mem'ries of the tales
   Of Edgar Allan Poe!
At last I got upon my feet,
   And staggered to the door —
The fatal door, which stood ajar —
   And trod the fatal floor.
I gazed adown the passage,
   Which was in deepest gloom,
And groped my way along its sides
   Until I reached the room.
With bloodshot eyes, and heated brain,
   I firmly clutched the knob,
When smote upon my list'ning ear
   A touching, piteous sob.
Oh, could it be, the ruffians,
   Their cruel purpose wrought,
Their deep remorse were sobbing forth
   In agonising thought?
No longer purposeless I stayed,
   But pushed the door aside,
And stood, in a sickening vapour
   Alone at the murd'rers' side.

While yet in the far-off corner
   Their blood-stained victim lay:
I'd, undefended, entered in
   To bring the fiends to bay;
When, all of a sudden, a woman
   Rose crying from where she sat,
And said, with the deepest emotion,
   'We've just had to kill our cat.'

Billy's rose
George R. Sims

Billy's dead, and gone to glory — so is Billy's sister Nell:
There's a tale I know about them were I poet I would tell;
Soft it comes, with perfume laden, like a breath of country air
Wafted down the filthy alley, bringing fragrant odours there.

In that vile and filthy alley, long ago one winter's day,
Dying quick of want and fever, hapless, patient Billy lay,
While beside him sat his sister, in the garret's dismal gloom,
Cheering with her gentle presence Billy's pathway to the tomb.

Many a tale of elf and fairy did she tell the dying child,
Till his eyes lost half their anguish, and his worn, wan features smiled:
Tales herself had heard hap-hazard, caught amid the Babel roar,
Lisped about by tiny gossips playing round their mothers' door.

Then she felt his wasted fingers tighten feebly as she told
How beyond this dismal alley lay a land of shining gold,
Where, when all the pain was over — where, when all the tears were
    shed—
He would be a white-frocked angel, with a gold thing on his head.

Then she told some garbled story of a kind-eyed Saviour's love,
How He'd built for little children great big playgrounds up above,
Where they sang and played at hop-scotch and at horses all the day,
And where beadles and policemen never frightened them away.

This was Nell's idea of Heaven — just a bit of what she'd heard,
With a little bit invented, and little bit inferred.
Her brother lay and listened, and he seemed to understand,
For he closed his eyes and murmured he could see the Promised Land.

'Yes,' he whispered, 'I can see it — I can see it, sister Nell;
Oh, the children look so happy, and they're all so strong and well;
I can see them there with Jesus — He is playing with them, too!
Let us run away and join them if there's room for me and you.'

She was eight, this little maiden, and her life had all been spent
In the garret and the alley, where they starved to pay the rent;
Where a drunken father's curses and a drunken mother's blows
Drove her forth into the gutter from the day's dawn to its close.

But she knew enough, this outcast, just to tell the sinking boy,
'You must die before you're able all these blessings to enjoy.
You must die,' she whispered, 'Billy, and I am not even ill;
But I'll come to you, dear brother, — yes, I promise that I will.'

'You are dying, little brother, — you are dying, oh, so fast;
I heard father say to mother that he knew you couldn't last.
They will put you in a coffin, then you'll wake and be up there,
While I'm left alone to suffer in this garret bleak and bare.'

'Yes, I know it', answered Billy. 'Ah, but, sister, I don't mind,
Gentle Jesus will not beat me; He's not cruel or unkind.
But I can't help thinking, Nelly, I should like to take away
Something, sister, that you gave me, I might look at every day.

'In the summer you remember how the mission took us out
To a great green lovely meadow, where we played and ran about,
And the van that took us halted by a sweet bright patch of land,
Where the fine red blossoms grew, dear, half as big as mother's hand.

'Nell, I asked the good kind teacher what they called such flowers as those,
And he told me, I remember, that the pretty name was rose.
I have never seen them since, dear — how I wish that I had one!
Just to keep and think of you, Nell, when I'm up beyond the sun.'

Not a word said little Nelly; but at night, when Billy slept,
On she flung her scanty garments and then down the stairs she crept.
Through the silent streets of London she ran nimbly as a fawn,
Running on and running ever till the night had changed to dawn.

When the foggy sun had risen, and the mist had cleared away,
All around her, wrapped in snowdrift, there the open country lay.
She was tired, her limbs were frozen, and the roads had cut her feet,
But there came no flowery gardens her poor tearful eyes to greet.

She had traced the road by asking — she had learnt the way to go;
She had found the famous meadow — it was wrapped in cruel snow;
Not a buttercup or daisy, not a single verdant blade
Showed its head above its prison. Then she knelt her down and prayed.

With her eyes upcast to heaven, down she sank upon the ground,
And she prayed to God to tell her where the roses might be found.
Then the cold blast numbed her senses, and her sight grew strangely dim;
And a sudden, awful tremor seemed to seize her every limb.

'Oh, a rose!' she moaned, 'good Jesus—just a rose to take to Bill!'
And as she prayed a chariot came thundering down the hill;
And a lady sat there, toying with a red rose, rare and sweet;
As she passed she flung it from her, and it fell at Nelly's feet.

Just a word her lord had spoken caused her ladyship to fret,
And the rose had been his present, so she flung it in a pet;
But the poor, half-blinded Nelly thought it fallen from the skies,
And she murmured, 'Thank you, Jesus!' as she clasped the dainty prize.

Lo that night from out the alley did a child's soul pass away,
From dirt and sin and misery to where God's children play.
Lo that night a wild, fierce snowstorm burst in fury o'er the land,
And at morn they found Nell frozen, with the red rose in her hand.

Billy's dead, and gone to glory — so is Billy's sister Nell;
Am I bold to say this happened in the land where angels dwell: —
That the children met in heaven, after all their earthly woes,
And that Nelly kissed her brother, and said, 'Billy, here's your rose'?

The dream of the bilious beadle
Arthur Shirley

'Twas in the grimy winter time, an evening cold and damp,
And four-and-twenty workus boys, all one poor ill-fed stamp,
Were blowing on blue finger-tips, bent double with the cramp;
And when the skilly poured out fell into each urchin's pan,
They swallowed it at such a rate as only boyhood can.
But the Beadle sat remote from all, a bilious-looking man —
His hat was off, red vest apart, to catch the evening breeze.
He thought that this would cool his brow; it only made him sneeze;
So he pressed his side with his hand, and tried to 'pear as if at ease.
Heave after heave his waistcoat gave, to him was peace denied;
It tortured him to see them eat — he couldn't though he tried!
Good fare had made him much too fat, and rather goggle-eyed.
At length he started to his feet, some hurried steps he took,
Now up the ward, now down the ward, with wild dyspeptic look,
And lo! he saw a workus boy, who read a penny book.
'You dreadful brat! what is't you're at? I warrant 'tis no good!
What's this? "The Life of Turpin Bold!" or "Death of Robin Hood!" '
'It's Hessays on the Crumpet, sir, as a harticle of food!'
He started from that boy as though in's ear had blown a trumpet;
His hand he prest upon his chest, then with his fist did thump it,
And then he sat beside the brat and talked about the crumpet.
How, now and them, that muffin men of whom tradition tells,
Fortunes had made by pastry trade, and come out awful swells,
While their old patrons suffered worse than Irving in "The Bells!"
'And well I know, forsooth,' said he, 'for plenty have I bought,
The sufferings of foolish folk who eat more than they ought.
With Pepsine Pills and Liver Pads is their consumption fraught.
Oh! oh! my boy! my pauper boy! take my advice—'tis best shun
All such tempting tasty things, though nice beyond all question,
Unless, like me, you wish to feel the pangs of indigestion!
One, who had ever made me long — a muffin man and old —
I watched into a public house, he called for whiskey cold,
And for a moment, left his stock within green baize enrolled.
I crept up to them, thinking what an appetite I'd got,
I gloated o'er them lying there elastic and all hot;

I thought of butter laid on thick, and then — I prig'd the lot!
I took them home, I toasted them, p'raps upwards of a score,
And never had so fine a feast on luscious fare before,
"And now," I said, "I'll go to bed and dream of eating more."
All night I lay uneasily and rolled from side to side,
At first without one wink of sleep, no matter how I tried;
And then I dreamt I was a 'bus, and gurgled "Full inside!"
I was a 'bus by nightmares drawn on to some giddy crest,
Now launched like lightning through the air, now stopt and now comprest;
I felt a million muffin men were seated on my chest!
I heard their bells — their horrid bells — in sound as loud as trumpets,
Oh, curses on ye, spongy tribe! ye cruffins and ye mumpets! —
I must be mad! I mean to say, ye muffins and ye crumpets!
Then came a chill like Wenham ice; then hot as hottest steam;
I could not move a single limb! I could not even scream!
You pauper brat, remember that all this was but a dream!'
The boy gazed on his troubled brow, from which big drops were oozing,
And, for a moment all respect for his dread function losing,
Made this remark—'Well, blow me tight, our Beadle's been a-boozing!'
That very week, before the beak they brought that beadle burly;
He pleaded guilty in a tone dyspeptically surly,
And he lives at Pentonville, with hair not long or curly!

The green eye of the Yellow God
J. Milton Hayes

There's a one-eyed yellow idol to the north of Khatmandu,
There's a little marble cross below the town;
There's a broken-hearted woman tends the grave of Mad Carew,
And the Yellow God forever gazes down.

He was known as 'Mad Carew' by the subs at Khatmandu,
He was hotter than they felt inclined to tell;
But for all his foolish pranks, he was worshipped in the ranks,
And the Colonel's daughter smiled on him as well.

He had loved her all along, with a passion of the strong,
The fact that she loved him was plain to all.
She was nearly twenty-one and arrangements had begun
To celebrate her birthday with a ball.

He wrote to ask what present she would like from Mad Carew;
They met next day as he dismissed a squad;
And jestingly she told him then that nothing else would do
But the green eye of the little Yellow God.

On the night before the dance, Mad Carew seemed in a trance,
And they chaffed him as they puffed at their cigars;
But for once he failed to smile, and he sat alone awhile,
Then went out into the night beneath the stars.

He returned before the dawn, with his shirt and tunic torn,
And a gash across his temple dripping red;
He was patched up right away, and he slept through all the day,
And the Colonel's daughter watched beside his bed.

He woke at last and asked if they could send his tunic through;
She brought it, and he thanked her with a nod;
He bade her search the pocket saying, 'That's from Mad Carew',
And she found the little green eye of the god.

She upbraided poor Carew in the way that women do,
Though both her eyes were strangely hot and wet;
But she wouldn't take the stone and Mad Carew was left alone
With the jewel that he'd chanced his life to get.

When the ball was at its height, on that still and tropic night,
She thought of him and hastened to his room;
As she crossed the barrack square she could hear the dreamy air
Of a waltz tune softly stealing thro' the gloom.

His door was open wide, with silver moonlight shining through;
The place was wet and slipp'ry where she trod;
An ugly knife lay buried in the heart of Mad Carew,
'Twas the 'Vengeance of the Little Yellow God'.

There's a one-eyed yellow idol to the north of Khatmandu,
There's a little marble cross below the town;
There's a broken-hearted woman tends the grave of Mad Carew,
And the Yellow God forever gazes down.

How I won my wife's heart
Will Carleton

A handsome night, with the trees snow-white,
    And the time say ten or more,
Saw wife and me, with a well-fed glee,
    Drive home from Jackson's store.
As we trotted along, our two-thread song
    Wove in with the sleigh-bell's chimes;
Our laugh ran free, and it seemed to me
    We was havin' first-rate times.
I said 'first-rate', but I do not say it
    On a thoroughly-thorough plan;
I had won my wife, in legitimate strife,
    Away from her first young man.
'Twas a perfect rout, and a fair cut out,
    With nothing sneaky or wrong;
But I wondered as to whether or no
    She had brought her heart along!
A woman half-won is worse than none,
    With another man keepin' part;
It's nothin' to gain her body and brain,
    If she can't throw in her heart.
And I felt and thought that I sometimes caught
    A chillness out of her mind;
She was too much prone to thinkin' alone,
    And rather too coldly kind.
But things seemed right this partic'lar night,
    And better than average folks;
And we filled the air with music to spare
    And complimentary jokes.
Till, as I reckoned, about a second
    All happened to be still —
A cry like the yell of hounds from hell
    Came over a neighbouring hill.
It cut like a blade through the leafless shade,
    It chilled us stiff with dread;

We looked loud cries in each other's eyes—
   And — 'Wolves!' was all we said!
And this was a year with a winter more drear
   Than any we'd ever known;
It was '43; and the wolves, you see,
   Had a famine of their own.
That season, at least, of man and beast
   They had captured many a one;
And we knew, by the sound of their voice that night,
   That they hadn't come out for fun.
My horses felt need of all their speed,
   And every muscle strained;
But, all they could do, I felt and knew
   That the hungry devils gained.
'Twas but two miles more to our own house door,
   Where shelter we would find,
When I saw the pack close on to our tracks,
   Not a hundred yards behind.
Then I says to my wife, 'Now drive for life!
   They're a-comin' over-nigh!
And I will stand, gun and axe in hand,
   And be the first to die.'
As the reins she took, she gave me a look
   Sweet memory makes long-lived;
I thought, 'I'll allow she loves me now;
   The rest of her heart has arrived.'
I felt I could fight the whole of the night,
   And never flinch or tire!
In danger, mind you, a woman behind you
   Can turn your blood to fire.
When they reached the right spot, I left 'em a shot,
   But it wasn't a steady aim—
'Twasn't really mine — and they tips me a whine,
   And came on all the same.
Their leader sped a little ahead
   Like a grey knife from its sheath;
With a resolute eye, and a hungry cry,
   And an excellent set of teeth.
A moment I gazed — my axe I raised —

It hissed above my head —
Crunching low and dull, it split his skull,
    And the villain fell back dead!
It checked them there, and a minute to spare
    We had, and a second besides;
With rites unsaid they buried their dead
    In the graves of their own lank hides.
They made for him a funeral grim —
    Himself the unbaked meat;
And when they were through with their barbecue
    They started for more to eat!
With voices aflame, once more they came;
    But faster still we sped,
And we and our traps dashed home perhaps
    A half-minute ahead.
My wife I bore through the open door,
    Then turned to the hearth clean swept,
Where a log-fire glowed in its brick abode
    By my mother faithfully kept;
From the hearth raising two faggots blazing,
    I leapt like lightning back;
I dashed the brands, with my blistering hands,
    In the teeth of the howling pack.
They shrank with fright from the feel and sight
    Of this sudden volley of flame;
With a yell of dread, they sneaked and fled,
    As fast as they ever came.
As I turned around, my wife I found
    Not the eighth of an inch away;
She looked so true and tender, I knew
    That her heart had come — to stay.
She nestled more nigh, with love-lit eye
    And passionate-quivering lip;
And I saw that the lout whom I'd cut out
    Had probably lost his grip.
Doubt moved away, for a permanent stay,
    And never was heard of more!
My soul must own that it had not known
    The soul of my wife before.

As I staunched the steam on my foaming team.
  These thoughts hitched to my mind;
Below or above some woman's love,
  How little in life we find!
A man will go far to plant a star
  Where fame's wide sky is thrown,
But a longer way for some woman to say—
  'I love you for my own!'
Be't great or small — nine-tenths of all
  Of every trade and art,
Be't right or wrong — is merely a song
  To win some woman's heart.

Lasca
Frank Desprez

It's all very well to write reviews,
And carry umbrellas, and keep dry shoes,
And say what every one's saying here,
And wear what every one else must wear;
But to-night I'm sick of the whole affair,
I want free life and I want fresh air;
And I sigh for the canter after the cattle,
The crack of the whips like shots in a battle,
The melley of horns and hoofs and heads
That wars and wrangles and scatters and spreads;
The green beneath, and the blue above;
And dash and danger, and life and love.

And Lasca!

Lasca used to ride
On a mouse-grey mustang close to my side.
With blue serape and bright-belled spur;
I laughed with joy as I looked at her!
Little knew she of books or of creeds —
An Ave Maria sufficed her needs;
Little she cared, save to be by my side,
To ride with me, and ever to ride,
From San Saba's shore to Lavaca's tide.
She was as bold as the billows that beat,
She was as wild as the breezes that blow;
From her little head to her little feet,
She was swayed in her suppleness to and fro
By each gust of passion: a sapling pine,
That grows on the edge of a Kansas bluff,
And wars with the wind when the weather is rough,
Is like this Lasca, this love of mine.
She would hunger that I might eat,
Would take the bitter and leave me the sweet;
But once, when I made her jealous for fun,

At something I'd whispered, or looked, or done,
One Sunday in San Antonio,
To a glorious girl on the Alamo,
She drew from her garter a dear little dagger,
And — sting of a wasp! — it made me stagger!
An inch to the left, or an inch to the right,
And I shouldn't be maundering here tonight!
But she sobbed, and, sobbing, so swiftly bound
Her torn reboso about the wound,
That I quite forgave her. Scratches don't count
      In Texas, down by the Rio Grande.

Her eye was brown — a deep, deep brown;
Her hair was darker than her eye;
And something in her smile and frown,
Curled crimson lip, and instep high,
Showed that there ran in each blue vein,
Mixed with the milder Aztec strain,
The vigorous vintage of Old Spain.
She was alive in every limb
With feeling, to the finger-tips;
And when the sun is like a fire,
And sky one shining soft sapphire,
One does not drink in little sips.

Why did I leave the fresh and the free,
That suited her and suited me?
Listen awhile, and you will see;
But this be sure — in earth or air,
God and God's laws are everywhere,
And Nemesis comes with a foot as fleet
On the Texas trail as in Regent Street.

The air was heavy, the night was hot,
I sat by her side, and forgot — forgot:
Forgot the herd that were taking their rest,
Forgot that the air was close opprest,
That the Texas Norther comes sudden and soon,
In the dead of night or the blaze of noon;

That once let the herd at its breath take fright,
Nothing on earth can stop their flight;
And woe to the rider, and woe to the steed,
Who falls in front of their mad stampede!

Was that thunder? No, by the Lord!
I spring to my saddle without a word.
One foot on mine, and she clung behind.
Away! on a hot chase down the wind!
But never was fox-hunt half so hard,
And never was steed so little spared,
For we rode for our lives. You shall hear how we fared
     In Texas, down by the Rio Grande.

The mustang flew, and we urged him on:
There was one chance left, and you have but one:
Halt, jump to ground, and shoot your horse;
Crouch under his carcase, and take your chance;
And if the steers in their frantic course
Don't batter you both to pieces at once,
You may thank your stars; if not, good-bye
To the quickening kiss and the long-drawn sigh,
And the open air and the open sky,
     In Texas, down by the Rio Grande!

The cattle gained on us, and, just as I felt
For my old six-shooter behind in my belt,
Down came the mustang, and down came we,
Clinging together, and — what was the rest?
A body that spread itself on my breast,
Two arms that shielded my dizzy head,
Two lips that hard on my lips were prest:
Then came thunder in my ears,
As over us surged the sea of steers,
Blows that beat blood into my eyes,
And when I could rise,
Lasca was dead.

I gouged out a grave a few feet deep,
And there in Earth's arms I laid her to sleep.
And there she is lying, and no one knows,
And the summer shines and the winter snows,
For many a day the flowers have spread
A pall of petals over her head;
And the little grey hawk hangs aloft in the air,
And the sly coyote trots here and there,
And the black snake glides and glitters and slides
Into a rift in a cotton-wood tree;
And the buzzard sails on,
And comes and is gone,
Stately and still, like a ship at sea;
And I wonder why I do not care
For things that are like the things that were.
Does half my heart lie buried there
            In Texas, down by the Rio Grande?

The Pobble who has no toes
Edward Lear

The Pobble who has no toes
  Had once as many as we;
When they said, 'Some day you may lose them all';—
  He replied, — 'Fish fiddle de-dee!'
And his Aunt Jobiska made him drink,
Lavender water tinged with pink,
For she said, 'The World in general knows
There's nothing so good for a Pobble's toes!'

The Pobble who has no toes
  Swam across the Bristol Channel;
But before he set out he wrapped his nose,
  In a piece of scarlet flannel.
For his Aunt Jobiska said, 'No harm
Can come to his toes if his nose is warm;
And it's perfectly known that a Pobble's toes
Are safe, — provided he minds his nose.'

The Pobble swam fast and well,
  And when boats or ships came near him
He tinkledy-binkledy-winkled a bell,
  So that all the world could hear him.
And all the Sailors and Admirals cried,
When they saw him nearing the further side, —
'He has gone to fish, for his Aunt Jobiska's
Runcible Cat with crimson whiskers!'

But before he touched the shore,
  The shore of the Bristol Channel,
A sea-green Porpoise carried away
  His wrapper of scarlet flannel.
And when he came to observe his feet,
Formerly garnished with toes so neat,
His face at once became forlorn
On perceiving that all his toes were gone!

And nobody ever knew
   From that dark day to the present,
Whoso had taken the Pobble's toes,
   In a manner so far from pleasant.
Whether the shrimps or crawfish gray,
Or crafty Mermaids stole them away —
Nobody knew; and nobody knows
How the Pobble was robbed of his twice five toes.

The Pobble who has no toes
   Was placed in a friendly bark,
And they rowed him back, and carried him up,
   To his Aunt Jobiska's park.
And she made him a feast at his earnest wish
Of eggs and buttercups fried with fish;—
And she said, — 'It's a fact the whole world knows,
That Pobbles are happier without their toes'.

Santa Claus
Sophia Snow

'Twas the eve before Christmas; good-night had been said,
And Annie and Willie had crept into bed.
There were tears on their pillows, and tears in their eyes,
And each little bosom was heaving with sighs;
For to-night their stern father's command had been given
That they should retire precisely at seven
Instead of at eight; for they troubled him more
With questions unheard of than ever before.
He had told them he thought this delusion a sin;
No such creature as Santa Claus ever had been;
And he hoped, after this, he should never more hear
How he scrambled down chimneys with presents each year.
And this was the reason that two little heads
So restlessly tossed on their soft, downy beds.
Eight, nine, and the clock on the steeple tolled ten,
Not a word had been spoken by either till then;
When Willie's sad face from the blanket did peep,
And whispered: 'Dear Annie, is 'ou fast asleep?'
'Why, no, brother Willie,' a sweet voice replies:
'I've long tried in vain, but I can't shut my eyes;
For somehow it makes me so sorry because
Dear papa has said there is no Santa Claus.
Now *we* know there is, and it can't be denied,
For he came every year before dear mama died;
But, then, I've been thinking that she used to pray, —
And God would hear everything mama would say,—
And maybe she asked Him to send Santa Claus here
With the sack full of presents he brought every year.'
'Well, why tan'ot we p'ay, dust as mama did, den,
And ask Dod to send him wis presents aden?'
'I've been thinking so, too;' and, without a word more,
Four bare little feet bounded out on the floor,
And four little knees on the soft carpet pressed,
And two tiny hands were close clasped to each breast:—
'Now, Willie, you know we must firmly believe

That the presents we ask for we are sure to receive;
You must wait just as still till I say the "Amen",
And by that you will know that your turn has come then:—
"Dear Jesus, look down on my brother and me,
And grant us the favours we're asking of Thee.
I want a wax dolly, a tea-set and ring,
And an ebony workbox that shuts with a spring;
Bless papa, dear, Jesus, and cause him to see
That Santa Claus loves us as much as does he;
Don't let him get fretful and angry again
At dear brother Willie and Annie. Amen." '
'Please, Desus, 'et Santa Taus tum doen to-night,
And bring us some presents before it is 'ight;
I want he sood div' me a nice little sed,
With bright shinin' 'unners, and all painted 'ed;
A box full of tandy, a book and a toy,
Amen, and den, Desus, I'll be a dood boy.'

Their prayers being ended, they raised up their heads,
And with hearts light and cheerful, again sought their beds;
They were soon lost in slumber both peaceful and deep,
And with fairies in dreamland were roaming in sleep.
Eight, nine, and the little French clock had struck ten
Ere the father had thought of his children again;
He seems now to hear Annie's self-suppressed sighs,
And to see the big tears stand in Willie's blue eyes.
'I was harsh with my darlings,' he mentally said
'And should not have sent them so early to bed;
But then I was troubled; my feelings found vent;
For bank stock today has gone down two per cent;
But, of course, they've forgotten their troubles ere this,
And that I denied them the thrice asked-for kiss;
But just to make sure, I'll steal up to their door —
To my darlings I never spoke harshly before.'

So saying, he softly ascended the stairs,
And arrived at the door to hear both of their prayers.
His Annie's 'Bless papa' drew forth the big tears.
'Strange, strange! I'd forgotten,' he said, with a sigh,

'How I longed, when a child, to have Christmas draw nigh.
I'll atone for my harshness,' he inwardly said,
'By answering their prayers ere I sleep in my bed.'
Then he turned to the stairs and softly went down,
Threw off velvet slippers and silk dressing-gown,
Donned hat, coat and boots, and was out in the street,
A millionaire facing the cold, driving sleet!
Nor stopped he until he had bought everything,
From the box full of candy to the tiny gold ring.
Indeed, he kept adding so much to his store
That the various presents outnumbered a score.
Then homeward he turned, when his holiday load.
With Aunt Mary's help, in the nursery was stowed.

As soon as the beams of the bright morning sun
Put the darkness to flight, and the stars one by one,
Four little blue eyes out of sleep opened wide,
And at the same moment the presents espied.
Then out of their beds they sprang with a bound,
Then the very gifts prayed for were all of them found.
And they laughed and they cried, in their innocent glee;
And shouted for papa to come quick and see
What presents old Santa Claus brought in the night
(Just the things that they wanted!), and left before light.
'And now,' added Annie, in a voice soft and low,
'You'll believe there's a Santa Claus, papa, I know.'

Solitude
Ella Wheeler Wilcox

Laugh, and the world laughs with you:
Weep, and you weep alone;
For the sad old earth
Must borrow its mirth,
It has trouble enough of its own.

Sing, and the hills will answer;
Sigh, it is lost on the air;
The echoes bound
To a joyful sound,
But shrink from voicing care.

Rejoice, and men will seek you;
Grieve, and they turn and go;
They want full measure
Of all your pleasure,
But they do not want your woe.

Be glad, and your friends are many,
Be sad, and you lose them all;
There are none to decline
Your nectared wine,
But alone you must drink life's gall.

Feast, and your halls are crowded;
Fast, and the world goes by;
Succeed and give,
And it helps you live,
But it cannot help you die.

There is room in the halls of pleasure
For a long and lordly train;
But one by one
We must all file on
Through the narrow aisles of pain.

The yarn of the 'Nancy Bell'
W. S. Gilbert

'Twas on the shores that round our coast
   From Deal to Ramsgate span,
That I found alone on a piece of stone
   An elderly naval man.

His hair was weedy, his beard was long,
   And weedy and long was he,
And I heard this wight on the shore recite,
   In a singular minor key:

'Oh, I am a cook and a captain bold,
   And the mate of the Nancy brig,
And a bo'sun tight, and a midshipmite,
   And the crew of the captain's gig.'

And he shook his fist and he tore his hair,
   Till I really felt afraid,
For I couldn't help thinking the man had been drinking,
   And so I simply said:

'Oh, elderly man, it's little I know
   Of the duties of men of the sea,
But I'll eat my hand if I understand
   How you can possibly be

'At once a cook, and a captain bold,
   And the mate of the Nancy brig,
And a bo'sun tight, and a midshipmite,
   And the crew of the captain's gig.'

Then he gave a hitch to his trousers, which
   Is a trick all seamen larn,
And having got rid of a thumping quid,
   He spun this painful yarn:

''Twas in the good ship Nancy Bell
    That we sailed to the Indian sea,
And there on a reef we come to grief
    Which has often occurred to me.

'And pretty nigh all o' the crew was drowned
    (There was seventy-seven o' soul),
And only ten of the Nancy's men
    Said "Here!" to the muster-roll.

'There was me and the cook and the captain bold,
    And the mate of the Nancy brig,
And the bo'sun tight, and a midshipmite,
    And the crew of the captain's gig.

'For a month we'd neither wittles nor drink,
    Till a-hungry we did feel
So we drawed a lot, and accordin' shot
    The captain for our meal.

'The next lot fell to the Nancy's mate,
    And a delicate dish he made;
Then our appetite with the midshipmite
    We seven survivors stayed.

'And then we murdered the bo'sun tight,
    And he much resembled pig;
Then we wittled free, did the cook and me,
    On the crew of the captain's gig.

'Then only the cook and me was left,
    And the delicate question, "Which
Of us two goes to the kettle?" arose
    And we argued it out as sich.

'For I loved that cook as a brother, I did,
    And the cook he worshipped me;
But we'd both be blowed if we'd either be stowed
    In the other chap's hold, you see.

' "I'll be eat if you dines off me," says Tom,
    "Yes, that," says I, "you'll be,"—
"I'm boiled if I die, my friend," quoth I,
    And "Exactly so," quoth he.

'Says he, "Dear James, to murder me
    Were a foolish thing to do,
For don't you see that you can't cook *me,*
    While I can — and will — cook *you!*"

'So he boils the water, and takes the salt
    And the pepper in portions true
(Which he never forgot), and some chopped shalot,
    And some sage and parsley too.

' "Come here," says, he, with a proper pride,
    Which his smiling features tell,
"Twill soothing be if I let you see,
    How extremely nice you'll smell."

'And he stirred it round and round and round,
    And he sniffed at the foaming froth;
When I ups with his heels and smothers his squeals
    In the scum of the boiling broth.

'And I eat that cook in a week or less,
    And — as I eating be
The last of his chops, why, I almost drops,
    For a wessel in sight I see!

'And I never grin, and I never smile,
    And I never larf nor play,
But I sit and croak, and a single joke
    I have — which is to say:

'Oh, I am a cook and a captain bold,
    And the mate of the Nancy brig,
And a bo'sun tight, *and* a midshipmite,
    And the crew of the captain's gig!'

Yawcob Strauss
C. F. Adams

I haf von funny leedle boy,
　Vot gomes schust to mine knee;
Der queerest schap, der createst rogue
　As efer you dit see.
He runs und schumps und schmashes dings
　In all parts of der house:
But vot off dot? he vas mine son,
　Mine leedle Yawcob Strauss.

He gets der measles und der mumbs,
　Und eferyding dot's oudt;
He sbills mine glass of lager bier,
　Poots schnuff into mine kraut.
He fills mine pipe mit Limburg cheese, —
　Dot vos der roughest chouse:
I'd dake dot vrom no oder poy
　But leedle Yawcob Strauss.

He dakes der milk-ban for a dhrum,
　Und cuts mine cane in dwo,
To make der schticks to beat it mit, —
　Mine cracious, dot vos drue!
I dinks mine hed was schplit abart,
　He kicks oup sooch a touse:
But nefer mind; der poys vas few
　Like dot young Yawcob Strauss.

He asks me questions sooch as dese:
　Who baints mine nose so red?
Who vas it cuts dot schmooth blace oudt
　Vrom der hair ubon mine hed?
Und where der plaze goes vrom der lamp
　Vene'er der glim I douse?
How gan I all dose dings eggsplain
　To dot schmall Yawcob Strauss?

I somedimes dink I schall go vild
　Mit sooch a grazy poy,

Und vish vonce more I could haf rest
  Und peaceful dimes enshoy;
But ven he vash asleep in ped,
  So guiet as a mouse,
I prays der Lord, 'Dake anyding,
  But leaf dot Yawcob Strauss.'

You are old, Father William
Lewis Carroll

'You are old, Father William,' the young man said,
 'And your hair has become very white;
And yet you incessantly stand on your head —
 Do you think, at your age, it is right?'

'In my youth,' Father William replied to his son,
 'I feared it might injure the brain;
But, now that I'm perfectly sure I have none,
 Why, I do it again and again.'

'You are old,' said the youth, 'as I mentioned before,
 And have grown most uncommonly fat;
Yet you turned a back-somersault in at the door —
 Pray, what is the reason of that?'

'In my youth,' said the sage, as he shook his grey locks,
 'I kept all my limbs very supple
By the use of this ointment — one shilling the box —
 Allow me to sell you a couple?'

'You are old', said the youth, 'and your jaws are too weak
 For anything tougher than suet;
Yet you finished the goose, with the bones and the beak —
 Pray, how did you manage to do it?'

'In my youth,' said his father, 'I took to the law,
 And argued each case with my wife;
And the muscular strength which it gave to my jaw,
 Has lasted the rest of my life.'

'You are old,' said the youth, 'one would hardly suppose
 That your eye was as steady as ever;
Yet you balance an eel on the end of your nose —
 What made you so awfully clever?'

'I have answered three questions, and that is enough,'
  Said his father; 'don't give yourself airs!
Do you think I can listen all day to such stuff?
  Be off, or I'll kick you downstairs!'

7. GHOST STORIES

On a cold winter's night with the rain and the sleet and the snow coming down, there is no better way to pass the time than to read — or to be read — a ghost story. Here are three classics of the genre. They are to be read out loud at one sitting, with the lights turned low.

The adventure of the German student
Adapted from Washington Irving

On a stormy night, in the tempestuous times of the French Revolution, a young German was returning to his lodgings, at a late hour, across the old part of Paris. The lightning gleamed, and the loud claps of thunder rattled through the lofty, narrow streets—but I should first tell you something about this young German.

Gottfried Wolfgang was a young man of good family. He had studied for some time at Gottingen, but being of a visionary and enthusiastic character, he had wandered into those wild and speculative doctrines which have so often bewildered German students. His secluded life, his intense application, and the singular nature of his studies, had had an effect on both mind and body. His health was impaired; his imagination diseased. He had become haggard and desponding. His friends discovered the mental malady that was preying upon him, and determined that the best cure was a change of scene; he was sent, therefore, to finish his studies amidst the splendours and gaieties of Paris.

Wolfgang arrived in Paris at the breaking out of the French Revolution. The popular delirium at first caught his enthusiastic mind, and he was captivated by the political and philosophical theories of the day: but the scenes of blood which followed shocked his sensitive nature, disgusted him with society and the world, and made him more than ever a recluse.

While his mind was in this state, he had a dream which produced an extraordinary effect upon him. It was of a female face of transcendent beauty. So strong was the impression it made, that he dreamt of it again and again. It haunted his thoughts by day, his slumbers by night; in time he became passionately enamoured of this shadow of a dream. This lasted so long, that it became one of those fixed ideas which haunt the minds of melancholy men, and are at times mistaken for madness.

Such was Gottfried Wolfgang, and such his situation at the time I mentioned. He was returning home late one stormy night, through some of the old and gloomy streets of the Marais, the ancient part of Paris. The loud claps of thunder rattled among the high houses of the narrow streets. He came to the Place de Grève, the square where public executions are performed. The lightning quivered about the pinnacles of the ancient Hôtel de Ville, and shed flickering gleams over the open space in front. As Wolfgang was crossing the square, he shrunk back with horror at finding himself close by the guillotine. It was the height of the reign of terror, when this dreadful instrument of death stood ever ready, and its scaffold was continually running with blood of the virtuous and the brave. It had that very day been actively employed in the work of carnage, and there it stood in grim array amidst a silent and sleeping city, waiting for fresh victims.

Wolfgang's heart sickened within him, and he was turning shuddering from the horrible engine, when he beheld a shadowy form cowering as it were at the foot of the steps which led up to the scaffold. A succession of vivid flashes of lightning revealed it more distinctly. It was a female figure, dressed in black. She was seated on one of the lower steps of the scaffold, leaning forward, her face hidden in her lap, and her long dishevelled tresses hanging to the ground, streaming with the rain which fell in torrents. Wolfgang paused. There was something awful in this solitary monument of woe. The female had the appearance of being above the common order. He knew the times to be full of vicissitude, and that many a fair head, which had once been pillowed on down, now wandered houseless. Perhaps this was some poor mourner whom the dreadful axe had rendered desolate, and who sat here heartbroken on the strand of existence, from which all that was dear to her had been launched into eternity.

He approached, and addressed her in the accents of sympathy. She raised her head and gazed wildly at him. What was his astonishment at beholding, by the bright glare of the lightning, the very face which had haunted him in his dreams? It was pale and disconsolate, but ravishingly beautiful.

Trembling with violent and conflicting emotions, Wolfgang again accosted her. He spoke something of her being exposed at such an hour of the night, and to the fury of such a storm, and offered to conduct her to her friends. She pointed to the guillotine with a gesture of dreadful signification.

'I have no friend on earth!' said she.

'But you have a home,' said Wolfgang.

'Yes—in the grave!'

The heart of the student melted at the words.

'If a stranger dare make an offer', said he, 'without danger of being misunderstood, I would offer my humble dwelling as a shelter; myself as a devoted friend. I am friendless myself in Paris, and a stranger in the land; but if my life could be of service, it is at your disposal, and should be sacrificed before harm or indignity should come to you.'

There was an honest earnestness in the young man's manner that had its effect. The homeless stranger confided herself implicitly to the protection of the student.

He conducted his charge through the ancient streets of the *Pays Latin*, and by the dusky walls of the Sorbonne to the great, dingy hotel which he inhabited. The old portress who admitted them stared with surprise at the unusual sight of the melancholy Wolfgang with a female companion.

On entering his apartment, the student, for the first time, blushed at the scantiness and indifference of his dwelling. He had but one chamber—an old-fashioned saloon—heavily carved and fantastically furnished with the remains of former magnificence, for it was one of those hotels in the quarter of Luxembourg palace which had once belonged to nobility. It was lumbered with books and papers, and all the usual apparatus of a student, and his bed stood in a recess at one end.

When lights were brought, and Wolfgang had a better opportunity of contemplating the stranger, he was more than ever intoxicated by her beauty. Her face was pale, but of a dazzling fairness, set off by a profusion of raven hair that hung clustering about it. Her eyes were large and brilliant, with a singular expression that approached almost to wildness. Her whole appearance was highly striking, though she was dressed in the simplest style. The only thing approaching to an ornament which she wore was a broad, black band round her neck, clasped by diamonds.

In the infatuation of the moment Wolfgang avowed his passion for her. He told her the story of his mysterious dream, and how she had possessed his heart before he had even seen her. She was strangely affected by his recital, and acknowledged to have felt an impulse towards him equally unaccountable.

'Why should we separate?' said he: 'our hearts are united; in the eye of reason and honour we are as one. You have no home nor family, let me be everything to you, or rather let us be everything to one another. If form is necessary, form shall be observed—there is my hand. I pledge myself to you for ever.'

'For ever?' said the stranger, solemnly.

'For ever!' repeated Wolfgang.

The stranger clasped the hand extended to her: 'Then I am yours,' murmured she, and sank upon his bosom.

The next morning the student left his bride sleeping, and sallied forth at an early hour to seek more spacious apartments, suitable to the change in his situation. When he returned, he found the stranger lying with her head hanging over the bed, and one arm thrown over it. He spoke to her but received no reply. He advanced to awaken her from her uneasy posture. On taking her hand, it was cold—there was no pulsation—her face was pallid and ghastly. In a word—she was a corpse.

Horrified and frantic, he alarmed the house. A scene of confusion ensued. The police were summoned. As the officer of police entered the room, he started back on beholding the corpse.

'Great heaven!' cried he, 'how did this woman come here?'

'Do you know anything about her?' said Wolfgang eagerly.

'Do I?' exclaimed the police officer: 'she was guillotined yesterday!'

He stepped forward; undid the black collar round the neck of the corpse, and the head rolled on the floor!

The student burst into a frenzy. 'The fiend! the fiend has gained possession of me!' shrieked he: 'I am lost for ever!'

They tried to soothe him, but in vain. He was possessed with the frightful belief that an evil spirit had reanimated the dead body to ensnare him. He went distracted, and died in a madhouse.

The phantom coach
Adapted from Amelia B. Edwards

The circumstances I am about to relate to you have truth to recommend them. They happened to myself, and my recollection of them is as vivid as if they had taken place only yesterday. I entreat that you will abstain from forcing your own conclusions upon me. I want nothing explained away. My mind is quite made up, and, having the testimony of my own senses to rely upon, I prefer to abide by it.

It was just twenty years ago, and within a day or two of the end of the grouse season. I had been out all day with my gun, and had had no sport to speak of. The wind was due east; the month, December; the place, a bleak wide moor in the far north of England. And I had lost my way.

The snow began to come down with ominous steadiness, and the wind fell. After this, the cold became more intense, and the night came rapidly up. My heart grew heavy as I thought how my young wife was already watching for me through the window of our little inn parlour, and thought of all the suffering in store for her throughout this weary night. She had implored me to return before dusk, and I had promised her that I would. What would I not have given to have kept my word!

I stopped and shouted every now and then, but my shouts seemed only to make the silence deeper. Then a vague sense of uneasiness came upon me, and I began to remember stories of travellers who had walked on and on in the falling snow until, wearied out, they were fain to lie down and sleep their lives away. I shouted again, louder and longer, and then listened eagerly. Was my shout answered, or did I only fancy that I heard a far-off cry? I hallooed again, and again the echo followed. Then a wavering speck of light came suddenly out of the dark, growing momentarily nearer and brighter. Running towards it at full speed, I found myself, to my great joy, face to face with an old man and a lantern.

'Thank God!' was the exclamation that burst involuntarily from my lips.

'What for?' growled he, sulkily.

'Well—for you. I began to fear I should be lost in the snow.'

'Eh, then, folk do get cast away hereabouts fra' time to time, an' what's to hinder you from bein' cast away likewise, if the Lord's so minded?'

'If the Lord is so minded that you and I shall be lost together, friend, we must submit,' I replied; 'but I don't mean to be lost without you. How far am I now from Dwolding?'

'A gude twenty mile, more or less.'

'Where do you live, then?'

'Out yonder,' said he, with a vague jerk of the lantern.

'You're going home, I presume?'

'Maybe I am.'

'Then I'm going with you.'

The old man shook his head, and rubbed his nose reflectively with the handle of the lantern.

'It ain't o' no use,' growled he. 'He 'ont let you in—not he.'

'We'll see about that,' I replied, briskly.   'Who is He?'

'The master.'

'Well, well; you lead the way, and I'll engage that the master shall give me shelter and a supper tonight.'

'Eh, you can try him!' muttered my reluctant guide; and hobbled away through the falling snow. A large house loomed up presently out of the darkness.

Once inside, I looked round with curiosity, and found myself in a great raftered hall, which served, apparently, a variety of uses. One end was piled to the roof with corn, like a barn. The other was stored with flour-sacks, casks and all kinds of miscellaneous lumber. Presently a bell rang sharply.

'That's for you,' said my guide, with a malicious grin. 'Yonder's his room.

He pointed to a door at the opposite side of the hall. I rapped somewhat loudly, and went in. A huge, white-haired old man rose from a table covered with books and papers, and confronted me sternly.

'Who are you?' said he. 'How came you here? What do you want?'

'James Murray, barrister-in-law. On foot across the moor. Meat, drink, and sleep.

'Mine is not a house of entertainment,' he said, haughtily. 'By what right have you forced an entrance into it?'

'The right of self-preservation.'

'Self-preservation?'

'There's an inch of snow on the ground already,' I replied, briefly; 'and it would be deep enough to cover my body before daybreak.'

He strode to the window, pulled aside a heavy black curtain, and looked out.

'It is true,' he said. 'You can stay, if you choose, till morning. Jacob, serve the supper.'

A dish of ham and eggs, a loaf of brown bread, and a bottle of admirable sherry, were placed before me.

'I have but the homeliest farmhouse fare to offer you, sir,' said my entertainer. 'Your appetite, I trust, will make up for the deficiencies of our larder.'

I protested that I had never eaten anything so delicious. He bowed stiffly, and sat down to his own supper, which consisted of a jug of milk and a basin of porridge. We ate in silence, and, when we had done, I drew my chair back to the fireside. My host, somewhat to my surprise, did the same, and, turning abruptly towards me, said:

'Sir, I have lived here in strict retirement for three-and-twenty years. During that time I have not seen as many strange faces and I have not read a single newspaper. Will you favour me with a few words of information respecting that outer world from which I have parted company so long?'

'Pray interrogate me,' I replied. 'I am heartily at your service.'

He bent his head in acknowledgement; leaned forward, stared fixedly into the fire; and proceeded to question me.

His inquiries related chiefly to scientific matters, with the later progress of which he was almost wholly unacquainted. I replied as well as my slight information permitted; but the task was far from easy, and I was much relieved when, passing from interrogation to discussion, he began pouring forth his own conclusions upon the facts which I had been attempting to place before him. He talked, and I listened spellbound. He talked till I believe he almost forgot my presence, and only thought aloud. He spoke of the soul and its aspirations of the spirit and its powers; of second sight; of prophecy; of those phenomena which, under the names of ghosts, spectres, and supernatural appearances, have been denied by the sceptics and attested by the credulous of all ages.

'The world,' he said, 'grows hourly more and more sceptical of all that lies beyond its own narrow radius; and our men of science foster the fatal tendency. They condemn as fable all that resists experiment. They reject as false all that cannot be brought to the test of the laboratory or the dissecting-room. Against what superstition have they waged so long and obstinate a war, as against the belief in apparitions? And yet what superstition has maintained its hold upon the minds of men so long and so firmly? The evidence of competent witnesses, however conclusive in a court of justice, counts for nothing. He who pauses before he pronounces, is condemned as a trifler. He who believes, is a dreamer or a fool.'

He spoke with bitterness, and, having said thus, relapsed for some minutes into silence. Presently he raised his head from his hands, and added, with an altered voice and manner:

'I, sir, paused, investigated, believed, and was not ashamed to state my convictions to the world. I, too, was branded as a visionary, held up to ridicule by my contemporaries, and hooted from that field of science in which I had laboured with honour during all the best years of my life. These things happened just three-and-twenty years ago. Since then I have lived as you see me living now, and the world has forgotten me, as I have forgotten the world. You have my history.'

'It is a very sad one,' I murmured, scarcely knowing what to answer.

'It is a very common one,' he replied. 'I have only suffered for the truth, as many a better and wiser man has suffered before me.'

He rose, as if desirous of ending the conversation, and went over to the window.

'It has ceased snowing,' he observed, as he dropped the curtain and came back to the fireside.

'Ceased!' I exclaimed, starting eagerly to my feet, 'Oh, if it were only possible—but no! it is hopeless. Even if I could find my way across the moor, I could not walk twenty miles tonight.'

'Walk twenty miles tonight!' repeated my host. 'What are you thinking of?'

'Of my wife,' I replied, impatiently.

'Where is she?'

'At Dwolding, twenty miles away.'

'At Dwolding,' he echoed, thoughtfully. 'Yes, the distance, it is true, is twenty miles; but—are you so very anxious to save the next six or eight hours?'

'So very, very anxious, that I would give ten guineas at this moment for a guide and a horse.'

'Your wish can be gratified at a less costly rate,' said he, smiling. 'The night mail from the north, which changes horses at Dwolding, passes within five miles of this spot, and will be due at a certain cross-road in about an hour and a quarter. If Jacob were to go with you across the moor and put you into the old coach-road, you could find your way, I suppose, to where it joins the new one?'

'Easily—gladly.'

He smiled again, rang the bell and gave the old servant his directions.

I thanked him for his hospitality and would have shaken hands but that he had turned away before I could finish my sentence. In another minute I had traversed the hall, Jacob had locked the outer door behind me, and we were out on the wide white moor.

Although the wind had fallen, it was still bitterly cold. Not a star glimmered in the black vault overhead. Not a sound, save the rapid crunching of the snow beneath our feet, disturbed the heavy stillness of the night. Presently—at the end, as it seemed to me, of only a few minutes—Jacob came to a sudden halt, and said:

'Yon's your road. Keep the stone fence to your right hand and you can't fail of the way.'

'This, then, is the old coach-road?'

'Ay, 'tis the old coach-road.'

'And how far do I go before I reach the cross-roads?'

'Nigh upon three mile.'

I pulled out my purse, and he became more communicative.

'The road's a fair road enough,' said he, 'for foot passengers; but 'twas over-steep and narrow for the northern traffic. You'll mind where the parapet's broken away, close again' the sign-post. It's never been mended since the accident.'

'What accident?'

'Eh, the night mail pitched right over into the valley below—a gude fifty feet an' more—just at the worst bit o' road in the whole county.'

'Horrible! Were many lives lost?'

'All. Four were found dead, and t'other two died next morning.'

'How long is it since this happened?'

'Just nine year.'

'Near the sign-post, you say? I will bear it in mind. Good night.'

'Gude night, sir, and thankee.' Jacob pocketed his half-crown, made a faint pretence of touching his hat, and trudged back by the way he had come.

I watched the light of his lantern till it quite disappeared, and then turned to pursue my way alone. This was no longer matter of the slightest difficulty, for, despite the dead darkness overhead, the line of stone fence showed distinctly enough against the pale gleam of the snow. How silent it seemed now, with only my footsteps to listen to; how silent and how solitary!

Meanwhile, the night air seemed to become colder and colder, and though I walked fast I found it impossible to keep myself warm. My feet were like ice. I lost sensation in my hands, and grasped my gun mechanically. I even breathed with difficulty, as though, instead of traversing a quiet North-country highway, I were scaling the uppermost heights of some gigantic alp. This last symptom became presently so distressing that I was forced to stop for a few minutes and lean against the stone fence. As I did so I chanced to look back up the road, and there, to my infinite relief, I saw a distant point of light, like the gleam of an approaching lantern. I at first concluded that Jacob had retraced his steps and followed me; but even as the conjecture presented itself, a second light flashed into sight—a light evidently parallel with the first and approaching at the same rate of motion. It needed no second thought to show me that these must be the carriage-lamps of some private vehicle, though it seemed strange that any private vehicle should take a road professedly disused and dangerous.

There could be no doubt, however, of the fact, for the lamps grew larger and brighter every moment, and I even fancied I could already see the dark outline of the carriage between them. It was coming up very fast, and quite noiselessly, the snow being nearly a foot deep under the wheels.

And now the body of the vehicle became distinctly visible behind the lamps. It looked strangely lofty. A sudden suspicion flashed upon me. Was it possible that I had passed the cross-roads in the dark without observing the sign-post and could this be the very coach which I had come to meet?

No need to ask myself that question a second time, for here it came round the bend of the road, guard and driver, one outside passenger, and four steaming greys, all wrapped in a soft haze of light, through which the lamps blazed out, like a pair of fiery meteors.

I jumped forward, waved my hat, and shouted. The mail came down at full speed, and passed me. For a moment I feared that I had not been seen, or heard, but it was only for a moment.

The coachman pulled up; the guard, muffled to the eyes in capes and comforters, and apparently sound asleep in the rumble, neither answered my hail nor made the slightest effort to dismount; the outside passenger did not even turn his head. I opened the door for myself, and looked in. There were but three travellers inside, so I stepped in, shut the door, slipped into the vacant corner, and congratulated myself on my good fortune.

The atmosphere of the coach seemed, if possible, colder than that of the outer air and was pervaded by a singularly damp and disagreeable smell. I looked round at my fellow-passengers. They were all three men, and all silent. They did not seem to be asleep, but each leaned back in his corner of the vehicle, as if absorbed in his own reflections. I attempted to open a conversation.

'How intensely cold it is tonight,' I said, addressing my opposite neighbour.

He lifted his head, looked at me, but made no reply.

'The winter,' I added, 'seems to have begun in earnest.'

Although the corner in which he sat was so dim that I could distinguish none of his features very clearly, I saw that his eyes were still turned full upon me. And yet he answered never a word.

At any other time I should have felt, and perhaps expressed, some annoyance, but at the moment I felt too ill to do either. The icy coldness of the night air had struck a chill to my very marrow, and the strange smell inside the coach was affecting me with an intolerable nausea. I shivered from head to foot, and, turning to my left-hand neighbour, asked if he had any objection to an open window?

He neither spoke nor stirred.

I repeated the question somewhat more loudly, but with the same result. Then I lost my patience and let the sash down. As I did so, the leather strap broke in my hand, and I observed that the glass was covered with a thick coat of mildew, the accumulation, apparently, of years. My attention being thus drawn to the condition of the coach, I examined it more narrowly, and saw by the uncertain light of the outer lamps that it was in the last stage of dilapidation. Every part of it was not only out of repair but in a condition of decay. The sashes splintered at a touch. The leather fittings were crusted over with mould, and literally rotting from the woodwork. The floor was almost breaking away beneath my feet. The whole machine, in short, was foul with damp and had evidently been dragged from some outhouse in which it had been mouldering away for years, to do another day or two of duty on the road.

I turned to the third passenger, whom I had not yet addressed, and hazarded one more remark.

'This coach,' I said, 'is in a deplorable condition. The regular mail, I suppose, is under repair?'

He moved his head slowly, and looked me in the face, without speaking a word. I shall never forget that look while I live. I turned cold at heart under it. I turn cold at heart even now when I recall it. His eyes glowed with a fiery unnatural lustre. His face was livid as the face of a corpse. His bloodless lips were drawn back as if in the agony of death, and showed the gleaming teeth between.

The words that I was about to utter died upon my lips, and a strange horror—a dreadful horror—came upon me. My sight had by this time become used to the gloom of the coach, and I could see with tolerable distinctness. I turned to my opposite neighbour. He, too, was looking at me with the same startling pallor in his face and the same stony glitter in his eyes. I passed my hand across my brow. I turned to the passenger on the seat beside my own , and saw—oh, Heaven! how shall I describe what I saw? I saw that he was no living man— that none of them were living men. A pale phosphorescent light—the light of putrefaction—played upon their awful faces; upon their hair, dank with the dews of the grave; upon their clothes, earth stained and dropping to pieces; upon their hands, which were as the hands of corpses long buried. Only their eyes, their terrible eyes, were living; and those eyes were all turned menacingly upon me!

A shriek of terror, a wild unintelligible cry for help and mercy, burst from my lips as I flung myself against the door and strove in vain to open it.

In that single instant, brief and vivid as a landscape beheld in the flash of summer lightning, I saw the moon shining down through a rift of stormy cloud—the ghastly sign-post rearing its warning finger by the wayside—the broken parapet—the plunging horses—the black gulf below. Then the coach reeled like a ship at sea. Then came a mighty crash—a sense of crushing pain—and then darkness.

It seemed as if years had gone by when I awoke one morning from a deep sleep and found my wife watching by my bedside. I will pass over the scene that ensued and give you, in half a dozen words, the tale she told me with tears of thanksgiving. I had fallen over a precipice, close against the junction of the old coach-road and the new, and had only been saved from certain death by lighting upon a deep snowdrift that had accumulated at the foot of the rock beneath. In this snowdrift I was discovered at daybreak by a couple of shepherds, who carried me to the nearest shelter and brought a surgeon to my aid. The surgeon found me in a state of raving delirium, with a broken arm and a compound fracture of the skull. The letters in my pocket book showed my name and address; my wife was summoned to nurse me; and, thanks to youth and a fine constitution, I came out of danger at last. The place of my fall, I need scarcely say, was precisely that at which a frightful accident had happened to the north mail nine years before.

I never told my wife the fearful events which I have just related to you. I told the surgeon who attended me; but he treated the whole adventure as a mere dream born of the fever in my brain. We discussed the question over and over again until we found that we could discuss it with temper no longer, and then we dropped it. Others may form what conclusions they please—I *know* that twenty years ago I was the fourth inside passenger in that Phantom Coach.

The tell-tale heart
Adapted from Edgar Allan Poe

True! Nervous, very nervous I have been and am; but why *will* you say that I am mad? The disease had sharpened my senses, not destroyed, not dulled them. Above all was the sense of hearing acute. I heard all things in the heaven and in the earth. I heard many things in hell. How, then, am I mad? Hearken, and observe how healthily, how calmly I can tell you the whole story.

I cannot say how first the idea entered my brain; but, once conceived, it haunted me day and night. Object there was none. Passion there was none. I loved the old man. He had never wronged me. For his gold I had no desire. I think it was his eye! One of them resembled that of a vulture — a pale blue eye, with a film over it. Whenever it fell upon me, my blood ran cold; and so, by degrees, I made up my mind to take the life of the old man, and thus rid myself of the eye for ever. Now, you fancy me mad. But you should have seen me. You should have seen how wisely I proceeded — with what caution — with what foresight — with what dissimulation! I was never kinder to the old man than during the week before I killed him. And every night, about midnight, I turned the latch of his door and opened it—oh, so gently!—and when I had made an opening sufficient for my head, I put in a dark lantern — closed so that no light shone out— and then I thrust in my head. Oh, you would have laughed to see how cunningly, slowly, very, very slowly I thrust it in, so that I might not disturb the old man's sleep. It took me an hour to place my whole head within the opening so that I could see him in his bed. Ha! would a madman have been so wise as this? And then I undid the lantern *cautiously* — oh, *so* cautiously (for the hinges creaked) just so much that one thin ray fell upon the vulture eye. This I did for seven long nights; but I found the eye always closed; and so it was impossible to do the work; for it was not the old man who vexed me, but his evil eye. And every morning, I went boldly into the chamber and spoke to him in a hearty tone, inquiring how he had passed the night. So you see he would have been a very profound old man indeed to suspect that every night I looked in upon him while he slept. On the eighth night I was more than usually cautious in opening the door. I *felt* so proud of my sagacity that I could scarcely contain my feelings of triumph. To think that he did not even dream of my secret deeds or thoughts. I fairly chuckled at the idea; and, perhaps, he heard me, for he moved on the bed suddenly, as if startled. Now you may think that I drew back — but no. His room was as black as pitch with the thick darkness (for the shutters were fastened), and so I knew that he could not see the opening of the door, and I kept pushing it on steadily, steadily. I was about to open the lantern, when my finger slipped on the fastening, and the old man sprang up in the bed, crying out 'Who's there?' I kept quite still, for a whole hour, not moving a muscle, and all the time he was sitting up in the bed, listening.

Presently I heard a slight groan, and I knew it was the groan of mortal terror — the low, stifled sound that arises from the bottom of the soul when overcharged with awe. I knew the sound well, for many a night it had welled up from my own bosom, deepening, with its dreadful echo, the terrors that distracted me. I knew what the old man felt, and pitied him, although I chuckled at heart. I knew that he had been lying awake ever since the first slight noise, and his fears had been ever since growing upon him. He had been trying to fancy them causeless, but could not. Yes, he had been trying to comfort himself with all sorts of suppositions; but in vain. *All in vain*; because Death, in approaching him, had stalked with his black shadow before him, and enveloped the victim. And it was the mournful influence of the unperceived shadow that caused him, though he neither saw nor heard, to *feel* my presence in the room. After waiting a long time, very patiently, without hearing him lie down, I resolved to open a little — a very, very little — crevice in the lantern. This I did very stealthily — until at length a single dim ray shot out from the crevice and fell upon the vulture eye. It was open, wide open, and I grew furious as I gazed upon it. I saw with perfect distinctness — all a dull blue, with a hideous veil over it that chilled the very marrow in my bones; but I could see nothing else of the old man's face or person: for I had directed the ray, as if by instinct, precisely upon the damned spot.

And now there came to my ears a low, dull, quick sound, such as a watch makes when enveloped in cotton. I knew *that* sound well, too. It was the beating of the old man's heart. It increased my fury, as the beating of a drum stimulates the soldier into courage. But even yet I refrained and kept still. I scarcely breathed. I held the lantern motionless. I tried how steadily I could maintain the ray upon the eye. Meantime the hellish tattoo heart increased. It grew quicker and quicker, and louder and louder every instant; the old man's terror *must* have been extreme! I have told you that I am nervous; and now, at the dead hour of the night, amid the dreadful silence of that old house, so strange a noise as this excited me to uncontrollable terror. Yet, for some minutes longer I refrained and stood still. But the beating grew louder, louder! I thought the heart must *burst*. And now a new anxiety seized me—the sound would be heard by a neighbour! The old man's hour had come! With a loud yell I threw open the lantern and leaped into the room. He shrieked *once*—once *only*. In an instant I dragged him to the floor,and pulled the heavy bed over him. I then smiled gaily, to find the deed so far done. But, for many minutes, the heart beat on with a muffled sound. This, however, did not vex me; it would not be heard through the wall. At length it ceased. The old man was dead. I removed the bed and examined the corpse. Yes, he was stone, stone dead. His eye would trouble me no more. I took up three planks from the flooring, and deposited all between the scantlings. I then replaced the boards so cleverly, so cunningly, that no human eye—not even *his*—could have detected anything wrong. There was nothing to wash out—no stain of any kind—no blood spot whatever. I had been too wary for that.

When I had finished it was four o'clock—still dark as midnight. As the hour struck, there came a knocking at the street door. I went down to open it with a light heart — for what had I *now* to fear? There entered three men, who introduced themselves as officers of the police. A shriek had been heard during the night; suspicion of foul play had been aroused; information had been lodged at the police-office, and these men had been deputed to search the premises.

I smiled — for *what* had I to fear? I bade them welcome. The shriek, I said, was my own in a dream. The old man, I mentioned, was absent in the country. I took my visitors all over the house. I bade them search — search *well*. At last I led them to *his* chamber. I shewed them his treasures, secure, undisturbed. In my confidence I brought chairs into the room, and desired them *here* to rest, while I, in the wild audacity of my perfect triumph, placed my own seat upon the very spot beneath which reposed the corpse of the victim.

The officers were satisfied, my *manner* had convinced them. We sat easy and chatted of familiar things. But ere long, I felt myself getting pale and wished them gone. My head ached, and I fancied a ringing in my ears: but still they sat, and still they chatted. The ringing became more distinct — it continued and became more distinct. I talked more freely to get rid of the feeling; but it continued and gained definitiveness — until, at length, I found that the noise was *not* within my ears. But I talked more fluently, and with a heightened voice. Yet the sound increased — and what could I do? It was *a low, dull, quick sound — much such a sound as a watch makes when enveloped in cotton*. Yet the officers heard it not. I talked more quickly — more vehemently; but the noise steadily increased. I rose and argued, loudly and violently, about trifles; but the noise steadily increased. Why *would* they not go? I paced the floor to and fro, as if excited to fury by the observations of the men — but the noise steadily increased. O God! what *could* I do? I foamed — I raved — I swore! I swung the chair on which I had been sitting, and grated it upon the boards; but the noise rose over all and continually increased. It grew louder — *louder* — LOUDER! And still the men chatted pleasantly, and smiled. Was it possible they heard not? Almighty God! — no, no! They heard — they suspected — they *knew!* — they were making a mockery of my horror! But anything was better than this agony! Anything was more tolerable than this derision! I could bear those hypocritical smiles no longer! I felt that I must scream or die! — And now — again! — hark! louder! *louder!* LOUDER! —

'Villains!' I shrieked, 'dissemble no more! I admit the deed! — tear up the planks! — here, here! — it is the beating of his hideous heart!'

8. FIRESIDE THEATRE

When contemplating amateur theatricals at home, simplicity is all. You won't be able to rival the glories of Drury Lane and it's unlikely that you'll even be able to match the efforts of the local operatic society, so don't try.

Theatrical happenings come in all shapes and sizes and, if sensibly conceived and properly rehearsed, can give enormous pleasure, whatever their setting. Once you have decided that you definitely *do* want to attempt something more ambitious than an evening of charades, your first task is to come up with an idea that won't overstretch your resources.

One-act plays

With only a sitting-room or a dining-room or a small garden at your disposal, *Oklahoma* is probably out. And with only yourself, your parents and your next-door neighbours for a cast, *Ali Baba and the Forty Thieves* is perhaps not a good idea. However, don't despair. There *are* good plays, requiring very small casts, which can be produced on minute stages and as often as not last for only half an hour.

Unfortunately, a number of would-be theatrical home entertainers shy away from presenting one-act plays, feeling that there is something altogether too amateurish (and hence undignified) about the form. Certainly, the commercial record of one-act plays is chequered, but just because a play won't work in a playhouse in the West End, it doesn't mean that it can't work in a parlour in West Kensington.

Very few people realise that many of today's best writers have produced one-act plays. Here is a brief list of examples, all of them by well-known authors, all of them capable of being presented in the home for almost nothing:

Afternoon at the Seaside by Agatha Christie (Males 7, Females 5)
Albert's Bridge by Tom Stoppard (M10, F2)
Already It's Tomorrow by Lynne Reid Banks (M2, F2)
The American Dream by Edward Albee (M2, F3)
The Apollo de Bellac by Jean Giraudoux (M6, F3)
Before the Flood by A. A. Milne (M5, F5)
The Bishop and the Actress by William Douglas-Home (M1, F1)
Black Comedy by Peter Shaffer (M5, F3)
The Browning Version by Terence Rattigan (M5, F2)
The Chairs by Eugene Ionesco (M2, F1)
Collect Your Hand Baggage by John Mortimer (M6, F5)
The Collection by Harold Pinter (M3, F1)
Deadly Poison by Michael and Roland Pertwee (M4, F4)
Double Double by James Saunders (M3, F2)
Endgame by Samuel Beckett (M3, F1)
The Form by N. F. Simpson (M2, F2)
The Girl by William Trevor (M7, F6)
A Glass of Bitter by J. B. Priestley (M3, F2)
The Happy Journey by Thornton Wilder (M3, F3)
Lonesome-like by Harold Brighouse (M2, F2)
No Why by John Whiting (M4, F3)
The Old Lady Shows Her Medals by J. M. Barrie (M2, F4)
Playgoers by Arthur W. Pinero (M2, F6)
A Pot of Broth by W. B. Yeats (M2, F1)
A Provincial Lady by Ivan Turgenev (M5, F2)
Shelter by Alun Owen (M1, F1)
Spreading the News by Lady Gregory (M7, F3)
Still Life by Noel Coward (M6, F5)
Thinking Aloud by Emlyn Williams (M1, F1)
Two Gentlemen of Soho by A. P. Herbert (M5, F3)

In a list like the one above, containing as it does thirty different plays by thirty distinguished playwrights, there are bound to be several plays that are far too ambitious for most home entertainers, but nonetheless there will be one or two (particularly those calling for only a couple of actors) to match *your* requirements and *your* resources.

The only way to find out is to read them — or, at least, to flick through the ones that look likely. They can be borrowed from any good local library or from the British Drama League Library at the British Theatre

Association (9 Fitzroy Square, London W1P 6AE) and they can be bought through Samuel French Limited (26 Southampton Street, London WC2E 7JE). French's also supply a comprehensive *Guide to Selecting One Act Plays,* which includes a brief synopsis of all the plays listed as well as full details of the size of the cast and the technical requirements of the play.

Pantomimes

Instead of a one-act play, around Christmas you might prefer to present a seasonal pantomime. Almost certainly the sort of £150,000 spectacular the London Palladium stages every year will be beyond your reach, but you and your friends might be amused to try some kind of potted panto, requiring the most elementary sets and costumes, and a cast of perhaps four or five.

The British Pantomime Association (170 Clarence Gate Gardens, London NW1 6AR) has a unique collection of pantomime scripts suitable for home entertainers and if you're after something traditional, simple but funny, you couldn't do better than get hold of one of Fred Rome's inimitable 'Potted Pantos'. Rome was the pen-name of Frederick Herbert Toplis who, from 1925 until his death in 1957 at the age of eighty-two, produced hilarious potted versions of *Cinderella, Aladdin, Robinson Crusoe, Dick Whittington, Sinbad the Sailor, Bluebeard, Babes in the Wood, Little Bo Beep, Sleeping Beauty, The Queen of Hearts, Little Red Riding Hood* and *Goody Two Shoes.* His scripts have now been brought together in one volume and published as a 'Wolfe Old Time Stars' Book' and they are ideal for fireside presentation.

Minstrel shows

In the Victorian heyday of home entertainment 'nigger minstrelsy', as it was rather unpleasantly called, was one of the most popular forms of fun. A minstrel show was an elaborate affair, featuring a cast of seven, including the 'interlocutor' (usually known as Mr Johnson), a bass singer, a tenor and four 'corner-men' who sat at the side of the stage and cracked the most outrageous gags.

In those days the programme would last an hour or more, with the performers running through a whole repertory of songs and sketches and comic routines, but it is unlikely that anyone today, when even the popularity of the *Black and White Minstrels* on television is beginning to wane, would want to devote a whole afternoon or evening to this kind of home entertainment. However, for the sake of novelty or nostalgia, a short improvised routine and a simple song in the minstrel manner might be worth trying.

Solo entertainments

Sadly, many potential parlour Thespians are frustrated because they cannot persuade other members of their family or their friends to take part in their home-made amateur dramatics. If you happen to be someone who is yearning to act but is surrounded by people who don't mind sitting and watching but loathe the idea of actually doing anything, why not try to devise a solo entertainment?

All you have to do is find a famous personality, who has had something written about him and who has written a great deal, study the character and his writings, and devise an entertainment representing, say, half an hour or an hour in his company. A number of fine actors have tried this and enjoyed a huge success — Max Adrian as George Bernard Shaw, Micheal MacLiammoir as Oscar Wilde, Roy Dotrice as John Aubrey, Emlyn Williams as Charles Dickens, Cyril Fletcher as Lewis Carroll — and if you have the necessary time, patience and interest, and could come up with a character whose personality and writings were sufficiently varied to sustain an entertainment, you might be on to something very exciting.

Only by reading their biographies and studying their writings will you discover whether certain lives offer the right kind of material for a project of this sort, but among the many possibilities, here are a few examples, taken from fact and fiction, that might be worth investigating:

Dr Johnson (by courtesy of Boswell)	Benjamin Franklin
	A. P. Herbert
Samuel Pepys	Sherlock Holmes (by courtesy of
Hilaire Belloc	Dr Watson and Arthur Conan
Edward Lear	Doyle)
James Thurber	Rudyard Kipling
Mark Twain	Jane Austen
Hercule Poirot (by courtesy of Agatha Christie)	Dorothy Parker
	Beatrix Potter

Shakespeare

Once you have successfully presented a whole season of one-act plays, pantomimes, minstrel shows and solo entertainments, you will probably be impatient to stage a Shakespeare play in your sitting-room. It won't be easy but it can be done — particularly if your sitting-room happens to be located in a huge country mansion or an enormous Scottish castle.

For those who don't have the facilities (or the gall) to present a full-scale Shakespearian production at home, but who would nonetheless like to have a go at putting on something by our greatest playwright, the Bard has been thoughtful. As you will recall, in his play *A Midsummer Night's Dream* a group of eager amateurs stage an entertainment at court. In the theatre the amateurs' playlet, entitled *Pyramus and Thisbe*, never gets the attention it deserves because Shakespeare allows his courtiers to keep up a running commentary. The story of Pyramus and Thisbe, as retold by Shakespeare, makes a perfect one-act play for the home entertainer, so here — presented for the very first time without superfluous interruptions —it is: *Pyramus and Thisbe*, a new play by William Shakespeare.

PROLOGUE: If we offend, it is with our good will.
        That you should think, we come not to offend,
    But with good will. To show our simple skill,
        That is the true beginning of our end.
    Consider then we come but in despite.
        We do not come as minding to content you,
    Our true intent is. All for your delight
        We are not here. That you should here repent you,
    The actors are at hand and by their show
    You shall know all that you are like to know.

Enter PYRAMUS and THISBE, WALL, MOONSHINE, and LION

PROLOGUE: Gentles, perchance you wonder at this show;
        But wonder on, till truth make all things plain!
    This man is Pyramus, if you would know;
        This beauteous lady Thisbe is certain.
    This man, with lime and rough-cast, doth present
        Wall, that vile Wall which did these lovers sunder;

And through Wall's chink, poor souls, they are content
   To whisper. At the which let no man wonder.
This man, with lanthorn, dog, and bush of thorn,
   Presenteth Moonshine; for, if you will know,
By moonshine did these lovers think no scorn
   To meet at Ninus' tomb, there, there to woo.
This grisly beast, which Lion hight by name,
The trusty Thisbe, coming first by night,
Did scare away, or rather did affright;
And, as she fled, her mantle she did fall,
   Which Lion vile with bloody mouth did stain.
Anon comes Pyramus, sweet youth and tall,
   And finds his trusty Thisbe's mantle slain:
Whereat, with blade, with bloody blameful blade,
   He bravely broach'd his boiling bloody breast;
And Thisbe, tarrying in mulberry shade,
   His dagger drew, and died. For all the rest,
Let Lion, Moonshine, Wall, and Lovers twain
At large discourse, while here they do remain.

Exeunt PROLOGUE, PYRAMUS, THISBE, LION and MOONSHINE

WALL: In this same interlude it doth befall
That I, one Snout by name, present a wall;
And such a wall, as I would have you think,
That had in it a crannied hole or chink,
Through which the lovers, Pyramus and Thisbe,
Did whisper often very secretly.
This loam, this rough-cast, and this stone doth show
That I am that same wall; the truth is so:
And this the cranny is, right and sinister,
Through which the fearful lovers are to whisper.

Re-enter PYRAMUS

PYRAMUS: O grim-look'd night! O night with hue so black!
    O night, which ever art when day is not!
  O night, O night! alack, alack, alack,
    I fear my Thisbe's promise is forgot!

> And thou, O wall, O sweet, O lovely wall,
>> That standst between her father's ground and mine!
> Thou wall, O wall, O sweet and lovely wall,
>> Show me thy chink, to blink through with mine eyne!

WALL holds up his fingers

PYRAMUS: Thanks, courteous wall: Jove shield thee well for this!
                But what see I? No Thisbe do I see.
              O wicked wall, through whom I see no bliss!
                Cursed be thy stones for thus deceiving me!

Re-enter THISBE

THISBE: O wall, full often hast thou heard my moans,
                For parting my fair Pyramus and me!
             My cherry lips have often kiss'd thy stones,
                Thy stones with lime and hair knit up in thee.

PYRAMUS: I see a voice: now will I to the chink,
              To spy and I can hear my Thisbe's face.
             Thisbe!

THISBE: My love! thou art my love, I think.

PYRAMUS: Think what thou wilt, I am thy lover's grace;
             And, like Limander, am I trusty still.

THISBE: And I like Helen, till the Fates me kill.

PYRAMUS: Not Shafalus to Procrus was so true.

THISBE: As Shafalus to Procrus, I to you.

PYRAMUS: O, kiss me through the hole of this vile wall!

THISBE: I kiss the wall's hole, not your lips at all.

PYRAMUS: Wilt thou at Ninny's tomb meet me straight-way?

THISBE: 'Tide life, 'tide death, I come without delay.

Exeunt PYRAMUS and THISBE

WALL: Thus have I, Wall, my part discharged so;
               And, being done, thus Wall away doth go.

Exit WALL

Re-enter LION and MOONSHINE

LION: You, ladies, you, whose gentle hearts do fear
                   The smallest monstrous mouse that creeps on floor,
               May now perchance both quake and tremble here,
                   When lion rough in wildest rage doth roar.
               Then know that I, one Snug the joiner, am
               A lion fell, nor else no lion's dam;
               For, if I should as lion come in strife
               Into this place, 't were pity on my life.

MOONSHINE: All that I have to say is, to tell you that the lanthorn is the
               moon; I, the man in the moon; this thorn-bush, my
               thorn-bush; and this dog, my dog.

Re-enter THISBE

THISBE: This is old Ninny's tomb. Where is my love?

THISBE runs off

LION: *(roaring)* Oh ———

The LION shakes THISBE'S mantle, and exit
Re-enter PYRAMUS

PYRAMUS: Sweet Moon, I thank thee for thy sunny beams:
                   I thank thee, Moon, for shining now so bright;
               For, by thy gracious, golden, glittering gleams,
                   I trust to take of truest Thisbe sight.
                       But stay, O spite!

But mark, poor knight,
What dreadful dole is here!
Eyes, do you see?
How can it be?
O dainty duck! O dear!
Thy mantle good,
What, stain'd with blood!
Approach, ye Furies fell!
O Fates, come, come,
Cut thread and thrum;
Quail, crush, conclude, and quell!
O wherefore, Nature, didst thou lions frame?
Since lion vile hath here deflower'd my dear:
Which is — no, no — which was the fairest dame
That lived, that loved, that liked, that look'd with cheer.
Come tears, confound;
Out, sword, and wound
The pap of Pyramus;
Ay, that left pap,
Where heart doth hop: *(Stabs himself)*
Thus die I, thus, thus, thus.
Now am I dead,
Now am I fled;
My soul is in the sky:
Tongue, lose thy light;
Moon, take thy flight:

Exit MOONSHINE

PYRAMUS: Now die, die, die, die, die. *(Dies)*

Re-enter THISBE

THISBE: Asleep, my love?
What, dead, my dove?
O Pyramus, arise!
Speak, speak. Quite dumb?
Dead, dead? A tomb
Must cover thy sweet eyes.

These lily lips,
This cherry nose,
These yellow cowslip cheeks,
Are gone, are gone:
Lovers, make moan:
His eyes were green as leeks.
O Sisters Three,
Come, come to me,
With hands as pale as milk;
Lay them in gore,
Since you have shore
With shears his thread of silk.
Tongue, not a word:
Come, trusty sword;
Come, blade, my breast imbrue:

(Stabs herself)

THISBE: And, farewell, friends;
Thus Thisbe ends:
Adieu, adieu, adieu.

The settings

Whatever you are presenting, be it a Fred Rome pantomime or a
Shakespearian playlet, you will need a setting. So long as the acting is
convincing, the setting can be as simple as you like. Of course, it is nice if
you happen to have a sitting-room with double doors opening on to a
dining room, so that the performance can be given in one room with the
audience seated in the other, but so long as everyone can see and hear
what's going on it doesn't much matter where you perform. In fact,
performing in the middle of an ordinary room with the minimum of props
and scenery is quite the done thing in the professional theatre these days,
so there is no need to feel awkward if you have no alternative but to
perform like this at home.

Naturally, attempt to make your scenery as convincing or as evocative as
you can. What is probably more important than an elaborate set is
effective lighting. It doesn't need to be complicated, but it should
concentrate the eye of the spectator on to the acting area. Playing in a

room where the audience is getting as much light as the performers is difficult and distracting for both spectators and players, so, wherever possible, direct the light towards the stage.

The costumes

Dressing-up, of course, is a form of home entertainment in its own right and there are a lot of people who, though quite unwilling to take part in a play, will gladly supply the costumes for it. With pantomimes and minstrel shows, you can go to town and take advantage of any old bits and pieces you happen to have hidden away, and the more outrageous they are the better. In the case of period plays, you must do some research. All libraries boast one or two books on theatrical costume which will show you what the characters *should* wear and all you can then do is attempt to approximate the originals. Period costumes are very difficult to concoct out of old dusters and grandmother's wedding dress, so that rather than attempting the impossible, you could try approaching the local amateur dramatic society and seeing if they can help. And when presenting plays in modern dress — and almost *anything* can be presented in modern dress — there is only one golden rule: *don't overdo it.*

The make-up

The same golden rule applies to make-up. It is very tempting to run riot with the greasepaint, but at close quarters an over made-up actor merely looks ridiculous. If you do consider theatrical make-up essential, either because you are going to be powerfully lit and will be playing a character not your own age or because there's nothing you love so much as messing about with greasepaint, you would be well advised to invest in a series of Leichner Make-up Charts. Leichner's (436 Essex Road, London N1 3PL) are the world's finest producers of theatrical make-up and publish an invaluable collection of charts that will show you exactly how to make up like a haggard man or a stage butler or an Italian or an Arab or an oriental or a negro (should you be contemplating Othello). Here is what they recommend as the right make-up for young, middle-aged and elderly men and women (reproduced by kind permission):

Make-up for a young woman

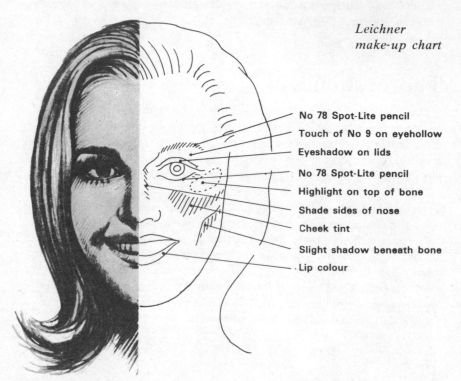

*Leichner
make-up chart*

No 78 Spot-Lite pencil

Touch of No 9 on eyehollow

Eyeshadow on lids

No 78 Spot-Lite pencil

Highlight on top of bone

Shade sides of nose

Cheek tint

Slight shadow beneath bone

Lip colour

This is a 'straight' make-up. Foundation, highlights, and shadows are used to accentuate your own features.

Foundation: Colouring must be selected according to type but No. 2 is a pale 'Dresden China' tint, No. 2½ a warm pink, No. 52 Peach Dark is a medium peach shade, and No. 53 Peach Special is a very effective deep peach.

Shading: No. 16 mixed with No. 25 Crimson Lake.

Highlights: No. 5 is generally most effective, but No. 2 or No. 20 (White) may be necessary under strong lighting.

Cheek colouring: No. 9 on cheekbone fading into Carmine 1 or Carmine 2 on fullness of cheeks.

Lips: Carmine 1, Carmine 2, or Carmine 3, sometimes with a little No. 20 (White) or No. 9 (Brick Red).

Eye make-up: Add touch of No. 9 to eyehollow (between eyelid and eyebrow). Use the Blue, Green, Mauve, Grey or Brown Eyeshadows on upper eyelids. Line eyes along line of lashes with No. 78 Spot-Lite Pencil and use the same pencil on eyebrows. Apply Mascara to lashes or use False Eyelashes.

Powder: Rose Blending Powder.

Apply Liquid Make-up to neck, hands and limbs.

Make-up for a young man

Leichner make-up chart

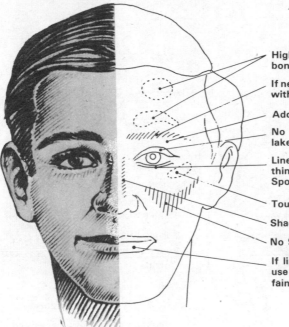

Highlight prominent parts of bone structure

If necessary, shape and colour with No 78 Spot-Lite pencil

Add touch of No 9 to eyehollow

No 16 mixed with No 25 crimson lake on eyelids

Line along line of lashes, thinly but sharply with No 78 Spot-Lite pencil

Touch of highlight on top of bone

Shade sides of nose

No 9 on cheeks

If lip colouring is necessary use No 9 very lightly — outlined faintly with No 25 crimson lake

This is a 'straight' make-up. Foundation, highlights and shadows are used to accentuate your own features.

Foundation: Colouring must be selected according to type but, as examples, No. 3½ gives a light tan, which can be deepened by adding No. 8 or No. 9, while No. 5 mixed with No. 9 gives a slightly yellow tan. No. 4 is a fairly deep reddish tan.

Shading: No. 16 Deep Brown mixed with No. 25 Crimson Lake.

Highlights: No. 5 is most effective although No. 20 (White) may be necessary under strong lighting.

Cheek colouring: No. 9 gives the most natural effect.

Lips: When lip colouring is necessary apply No. 9 lightly and outline with the faintest trace of No. 25 Crimson Lake.

Eye make-up: Add touch of No. 9 to eyehollow (between upper eyelid and eyebrow). Use No. 16 with No. 25 Crimson Lake on eyelids. Line eyes along line of lashes with No. 78 Spot-Lite Pencil and when necessary use same pencil on eyebrows.

Powder: Rose or Brownish Blending Powder.

Apply Liquid Make-up to neck, arms and hands.

Make-up for a middle-aged woman

Leichner make-up chart

- Highlights
- If necessary shape and colour with No 78 Spot-Lite pencil
- Shade inner corner of eyehollow
- Eyeshadow on lids
- Line eyes with No 78 Spot-Lite pencil
- Slight shadow under eyes
- No 9 or Carmine 2 on cheeks
- Slight shadow under cheekbone
- Slight shadows with highlights above
- Carmine 2

This is a mature face, still with some youthful features. Ageing should not be overdone. Facial colouring remains pleasantly warm and alive.

Foundation: Colouring must be selected according to type but as examples, No. 52 Peach Dark and No. 53 Peach Special are sophisticated shades, No. 2½ gives a medium pink complexion, while No. 6 is slightly sallow with a pink undertone.

Shading: No. 16 Deep Brown mixed with No. 25 Crimson Lake creating subtle pools of shadow accentuated with highlights.

Highlights: No. 5 is most effective although No. 2 or No. 20 (White) may be necessary under strong lighting.

Cheek colouring: No. 9, Carmine 1 or Carmine 2.

Lips: Carmine 2 or Carmine 3.

Eye make-up: The Blue, Green, and Mauve Eyeshadows are used on the eyelids when the characters are sophisticated, otherwise the Brown or Grey eyeshadows. Line eyes along line of lashes with No. 78 Spot-Lite Pencil, and apply Mascara to eyelashes, or use False Eyelashes.

Powder: Rose or Neutral Blending Powder.

Apply Liquid Make-up to neck, arms and hands.

Make-up for a middle-aged man

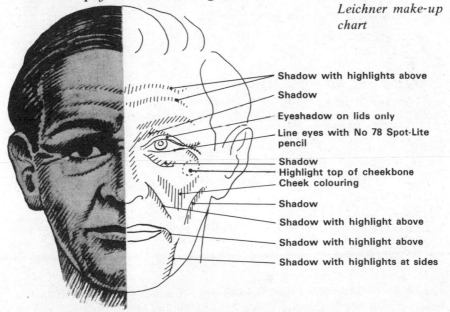

Leichner make-up chart

- Shadow with highlights above
- Shadow
- Eyeshadow on lids only
- Line eyes with No 78 Spot-Lite pencil
- Shadow
- Highlight top of cheekbone
- Cheek colouring
- Shadow
- Shadow with highlight above
- Shadow with highlight above
- Shadow with highlights at sides

This is a mature face, firm, still with some youthful features. Facial colouring remains pleasantly warm and alive.

Foundation: Colouring must be selected according to type but as examples No. 3½ with a little No. 9 gives a light normal skin tone, No. 4½ gives a rugged, outdoor tint, while No. 6 with a little No. 8 or No. 9 gives a healthy warm tint, with a slightly sallow undertone.

Shading: No. 16 Deep Brown mixed with No. 25 Crimson Lake, creating pools of shadow accentuated with highlights, not hard lines.

Highlights: No. 5 is most effective although No. 20 (White) may be necessary under strong lighting.

Cheek colouring: No. 25 Crimson Lake, sometimes also mixed with No. 9.

Lips: When lip colouring is necessary, apply No. 9 lightly and outline with the faintest trace of No. 25 Crimson Lake.

Eye make-up: Use shading material at inner corner of eyehollow, No. 16 mixed with No. 25 Crimson Lake, or No. 32 Dark Grey on eyelids. Line eyes along line of lashes with No. 78 Spot-Lite Pencil and if necessary use same pencil on eyebrows.

Hair: Slightly grey—use White or Light Grey Hair Powder. Streak hair at temples with No. 20 (White) Greasepaint or the Eau de Lys Liquid Make-Up White.

Powder: Rose or Brownish Blending Powder.

Make-up for an elderly woman

In the elderly face muscles and tissues sag, facial hollows deepen and folds of skin become pronounced. The skin tone is often sallow, frequently very delicate.

Foundation: No. 6 gives a sallow appearance with a slight pink undertone. Add No. 2½ for a healthier pink tone, or No. 9 for outdoor appearance. No. 5 with the addition of No. 59 Chrome Yellow will give a transparent, parchment effect.

Shading: No. 16 Deep Brown mixed with No. 25 Crimson Lake, or No. 25 Crimson Lake mixed with No. 31 Light Grey.

Highlights: No. 5 or No. 20 (White).

Cheek colouring: Carmine 2 or Carmine 3 lightly applied.

Lips: Carmine 3 lightly applied.

Eye make-up: Mauve shades of eyeshadow are most effective, or No. 16 mixed with No. 25 Crimson Lake. Line along line of lashes with No. 32

Use shading materials in natural furrows with highlights above, shade at temples

Whiten with No 22 white liner or No 31 light grey liner

Shade inner corner of eyehollow and highlight outer end to give drooping effect

Line along line of lashes with No 32 dark grey liner

Shadows with highlights between to give pouchy effect

Touch of Carmine 3

Shade under cheekbone

Ageing folds created by using shading material in furrows, with highlights above

Dark Grey, or with No. 25 Crimson Lake to give tired effect. Use No. 20 (White) or No. 31 Light Grey on eyebrows.

Hair: Use White or Light Grey Hair Powder. Streak with No. 20 (White) Greasepaint or Eau de Lys Liquid Make-up White.

Arms, neck and hands must be made-up in character.

Make-up for an elderly man

In the elderly face wrinkles and facial hollows deepen, muscles sag and the skin tone often looks sallow and blotchy.

Foundation: No. 6 is a sallow pink, useful for the ageing skin tone. Add No. 8 or No. 9 for a healthy ageing skin colour or add No. 25 Crimson Lake for a purplish complexion. No. 6½ is a sallow, olive tint.

Shading: No. 25 Crimson Lake, mixed with No. 16 Deep Brown or No. 32 Dark Grey.

Highlights: No. 5 or sometimes No. 20 (White) when the lighting is very strong.

Leichner make-up chart

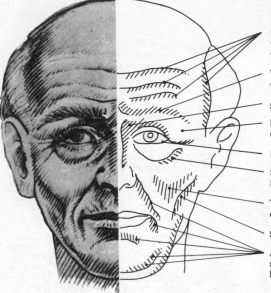

Use shading, in natural furrows with highlights above, shade at temples

Whiten with No 22 white liner or No 31 light grey liner

Shade inner corner of eyehollows

Highlight outer corner of eyehollow to give drooping effect

Line with No 25 crimson lake

Shadows with highlights between to give pouchy effect

Touch of No 25 crimson lake on cheeks

Shade under cheekbone

Ageing folds created by using shading material in furrows, with highlights above

Cheek colouring: No. 25 Crimson Lake.

Lips: Light application of No. 25 Crimson Lake.

Eye make-up: Use deep shadow at inner corner of eyehollow and highlight at outer end of eyehollow to create drooping effect, No. 25 Crimson Lake mixed with No. 16 Deep Brown or No. 32 Dark Grey on eyelids, and line along line of lashes with No. 32 Dark Grey or No. 25 Crimson Lake to give a bloodshot effect. Use No. 20 (White) or No. 31 Light Grey on eyebrows.

Hair: Use White or Light Grey Hair Powder. Streak with No. 20 White Greasepaint or Eau de Lys Liquid Make-Up White.

Powder: Rose or Neutral Blending Powder.

Remember to make up hands and neck in character.

9. SHOWTIME

A number of people are put off the idea of trying to become ventriloquists or puppeteers because they imagine the work involved will be too great. And others don't explore the possibilities of shadow shows and film shows at home because they suspect the expense will be considerable. Well, in both cases, of course, it *can* be — but it doesn't *need* to be. It you are prepared for effort and expense, you can do almost anything at home, but since this book isn't designed for dedicated fanatics, the emphasis in this chapter is on shows that can be staged successfully with the very minimum of preparation, equipment and skill.

Glove puppets

Throughout the United Kingdom, Sooty and Basil Brush are household names. The mischievous little bear with the heart of gold and the pun-loving fox with the outrageous laugh have become, in their own small ways, national figures with enormous followings. And yet they are only glove puppets, man-made dolls, with synthetic fur and glass eyes. The secret of their success, of course, is that their manipulators have given them very real personalities, so that when we see them on television or on the stage we believe in them as little creatures, with hearts and souls all their own.

The home entertainer who decides to present a puppet show must always bear this in mind. It is his job to persuade his audience that the puppets that clothe his fingers and thumbs are nothing to do with him. He must make the audience see them as self-sufficient animals or people with highly individual and independent personalities.

If he decides to present a Punch and Judy show this part of the job has already been done for him, because Mr Punch, the vigorous wife-beater with the voice of a deep-throated Donald Duck, and his raucously submissive wife Judy, have personalities that are already well-defined. Up until very recently, there were few British beaches that didn't boast at least one Punch and Judy booth, where children could sit and watch the familiar story being retold.

And it is vitally important when presenting Punch and Judy to get the story right. In essence it involves the hook-nosed hunch-backed Mr Punch being left at home to look after the baby while Judy goes out shopping. The baby, poor brute, begins to cry, cries louder when Punch attempts to soothe it and louder still when he decides to beat some sense into it. At last, infuriated by the baby, he flings it out of the window! Judy returns and is understandably furious; she attacks Punch who retaliates with vigour and manages to kill the poor lady. Punch now attempts to evade the law and in his flight encounters a series of characters—often including a doctor and a beadle and a crocodile—all of whom he fights and, as likely as not, kills. Eventually, the law catches up with him and he is sentenced to the gallows, where he cleverly tricks the hangman into putting his head through the noose and promptly manages to hang the hangman. Punch, now triumphant, is terrified by an encounter with the ghost of Judy and appalled to meet the Devil himself. However, he overcomes both in the end, and having beaten off all comers, takes his bow.

If you do decide to present Punch and Judy you will have to work out exactly how many of the characters you want to incorporate. Punch's friend the Clown, Punch's dog Toby, the doctor, the beadle, the crocodile, even Judy's ghost and the Devil, are all optional, but if you are going to attempt a traditional entertainment like this — it has been part of the British way of life since 1800 — you might as well go the whole way and do the job properly.

It is a grotesque story, but generations of children appear to have found the knockabout fun very much to their liking. Presenting it at home requires both skill and long practice: simply keeping the figure of Punch on the right hand for the length of the show is exhausting, never mind coping with the different puppets that must come off and on the left hand and mastering the extraordinary range of comic voices.

However, you may feel that 'His Highness of the Hump', as Punch was known for so many years, has had his day and that you would prefer to create a new story involving original characters. If you do, begin by defining for yourself the personalities of your central figures and the bare bones of the story. Impromptu puppetry simply does not work and trying to improvise the entertainment as you go along will only lead to disaster.

Having decided on the story and the characters, you must settle on a setting. With Punch and Judy it is traditional that the stage should be some six feet off the ground, so that the puppeteer stands with his hands above his head. With your own show, it will probably be simpler to cover an ordinary table with a table-cloth or sheet or blanket that reaches right down to the ground and sit hidden on one side of the table with the audience seated on the other.

If your show is going to involve a number of characters and a specific story, in the Punch and Judy manner, you will almost certainly need a few props. These should be placed on the stage by one of the puppets and not by a naked hand. It is probably a good idea to keep your hero on the stage all the time. This is easily done if you are wearing him on your right hand and have an assistant lurking behind the table with you to help you on and off with the other puppets and, should you want more than two characters on stage at a time, to actually don a puppet and join in.

Characters like Sooty and Basil Brush, of course, have human stooges. Sooty is often operated by his owner, Harry Corbett, and since Mr Corbett is no ventriloquist (not having had the benefit of this *Complete Book of Home Entertainment's* advice on ventriloquism) and appears on stage with Sooty while at the same time manipulating him, Sooty is unable to speak. Instead, he whispers in Mr Corbett's ear. This is a clever ploy and well worth imitating if you have no assistant ready to manipulate your puppet and yet want to appear on stage with him.

To do an act like that of Basil Brush, however, does require an accomplice, for Basil not only has a stooge but speaks as well. If you decide that you want to appear with your puppet or puppets, yet want him or them to speak, you will have to find someone prepared and able to manipulate them and speak for them from below the table while you are seen sitting at the table with them.

Glove puppets can be bought or made. The advantage of making your own is that you can give them appearances to match personalities you have chosen for them. The disadvantage is that it takes time and effort, though considerably less of both since the publication of Esme McLaren's book *Making Glove Puppets* (1973).

String puppets

All that has been said in the last chapter about amateur theatricals presented in the home applies to home-made marionette shows. The less ambitious you are, the more successful your entertainment will seem, and providing the show doesn't go on for too long, you the puppeteer don't appear and the puppets have real personalities and something specific to do, all should be well.

Constructing a proper theatre for marionettes can be complex and expensive. It's fun too, but if you have neither the patience nor resources to match the undertaking, you can easily make do with a very simple stage. What you must have is a front to your stage, in which the opening for the stage is just tall enough to give the puppets headroom and its width is sufficient to be in proportion, but the front as a whole is high enough for you to stand behind completely hidden and wide enough to allow for proper wings. Of course, if you simply stood behind a stage front designed like this the audience would be able to see your legs from the knees downwards, so a foot or so behind the proscenium you must erect a back wall for the stage (a curtain will do perfectly) which will hide your legs and over which you will lean to manipulate the marionettes.

Marionettes are difficult to make and easy to buy. As a compromise, if you happen to have dolls that are sufficiently flexible, you can in fact attach strings to them—one to each arm, one to each foot, one to the head—and use them as puppets. If you attach the strings for the feet to your thumb and little finger and the strings for the arms and head to the fingers in between, you will find that, with practice, it is quite possible to manipulate an ordinary doll—particularly one of the Action Man variety—as flexibly as any specially made marionette.

As far as the characters of the puppets and the story you choose to tell are concerned, the rules that apply to glove puppets apply to string puppets as well. Stage, scenery, marionettes, costumes and props can all be made at home, but if you want to present a professional marionette show, rather than the makeshift though entertaining kind described here, you should consult Benny Andersen's *Let's Start a Puppet Theatre* (1973) and Helen Binyon's *Puppetry Today* (1966).

Human puppets

As a one-man show, presenting a human marionette is hard to beat. All you need is a headless string puppet (or a decapitated doll with strings attached to its legs, arms and torso), your own face and an entertaining line in patter. The way to achieve the effect is better illustrated than described:

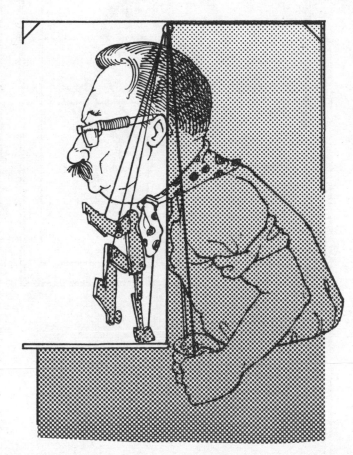

As you can see, your head appears above the puppet's body and while you chatter away you move the puppet's limbs by pulling on the strings which go over the top of the little proscenium and come down to where your hands are. The proscenium itself should be covered with a curtain with a hole in it through which you poke your head, so that the sight which greets the audience's astonished gaze will look something like this:

Toy theatres

The world of the toy theatre is an exciting one, but while you can set up a glove-puppet show or amuse your friends with a human marionette in an afternoon, preparing an entertainment for the toy theatre requires much more skill and specialist knowledge. Anyone can lurk behind a table and put a glove puppet on their right hand; almost anyone can attach strings to an old doll and make it dance; but not everyone can operate a toy theatre.

If you are intrigued by the possibilities of this unusual dramatic art form, you must do two things: read George Speaight's comprehensive *History of the English Toy Theatre* (1969) and visit Pollock's Toy Museum at 1 Scala Street, London WC1, where you can buy complete toy theatres, plus full instructions and selected scripts.

Black theatre

Black theatre is in no way related to the minstrel shows described in an earlier chapter. It is a form of entertainment that has become increasingly popular in recent years and is based on a simple illusion which gives the audience the impression that it is watching headless people and bodyless heads and all sorts of other amazing manifestations.

When presented on the professional stage, complicated lighting techniques, including the use of ultra-violet rays, are involved, but for home consumption the mechanics of black theatre are very much simpler. All you need is a small stage with a jet-black backcloth and wings where the performers can stand unseen before the entertainment begins. The stage itself is not lit, but there are lights on either side of the stage and these must *face the audience*. You don't want to blind the audience, but you must make sure that the lights — be they torches, gas lamps or reading lights — are pointing away from the stage and towards the auditorium.

What happens on stage is now up to you. Thanks to the black background and the lighting arrangements if you appear on stage dressed in black from top to toe, with black gloves on your hands and a black mask over your face, the audience will not be able to see you. This, of course, is how you engender the fun, for if you happen to carry a white cup and saucer on to the stage, from the audience's viewpoint the cup and saucer will appear to be floating!

The possibilities are endless, but should you choose to present a traditional black theatre show you will need three performers. The first will come on stage dressed in bright clothes as a Chinese magician. He will introduce himself as a famous magician and tell the audience that he can make men and women disappear. As he says this, on comes his assistant, again dressed in light clothes. First the magician makes the assistant's head disappear. This he does by throwing a white cloth over the assistant's head. When the cloth is removed, the assistant is standing there apparently headless. In fact, under the white cloth was a black cloth, and when the magician removed one but not the other, the audience saw the assistant with his head hidden by the black cloth and consequently he appeared beheaded.

Next the magician covers the assistant's body with a white cloak, and, hey presto! the moment the cloak is removed, we find the assistant has disappeared. The act continues with the magician promising further mysteries and his two assistants, invisible because they are dressed in black, performing them.

With black theatre you can make furniture float, ladders walk, pictures dance, skeletons glide and Ann Boleyn appear with her head tucked underneath her arm. It is important that the invisible performers remain as quiet as possible and advisable to keep domestic presentations of this kind as short as you can. It doesn't take long for the audience's eyes to become accustomed to the unusual light and discern the shadowy figures on the stage.

Shadow play

It is extraordinary the number of magical effects that can be created from the interplay of light and dark. With a well-placed torch or lamp or candle, you can create the most intriguing shadows. If you sling a sheet across the room and stand a light about five feet behind it, the figures who walk between the sheet and the source of light will cast dramatic shadows on to the sheet that can look most effective when viewed from the other side.

To create figures with your hands you don't even need a sheet. If you position your hands between the source of light and a blank wall, you will cast a shadow that can be turned to very entertaining effect. Experimenting will show you what can be done, but to get you started here are a few ideas for figures, complete with illustrations of the precise hand positions necessary to achieve the desired shadow.

Here is a wolfhound:

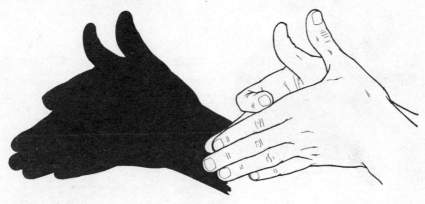

Here is the Hound of the Baskervilles:

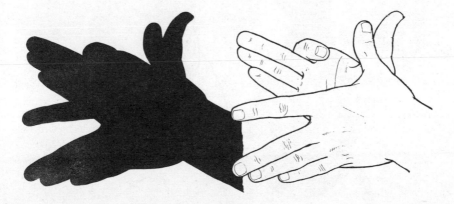

Here is a rabbit:

Here, with the aid of a carefully placed scarf or handkerchief, is a cat:

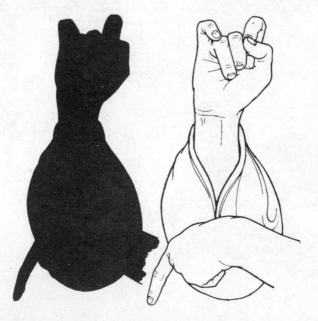

Here is a butterfly — or perhaps it's a china duck flying up the sitting-room wall:

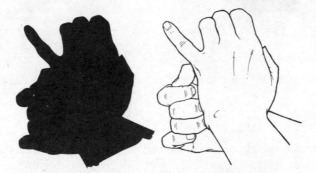

Here is a yokel wearing a crumpled country bumpkin's hat:

Here is Jacques Tati impersonating Monsieur Hulot:

And finally here's a bird you can end your act with. As you present this one, you explain to your audience that this is your swan-song:

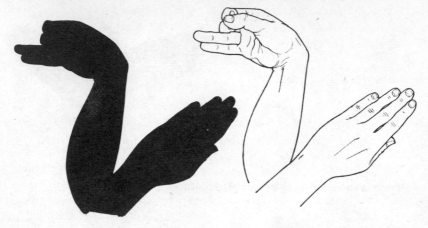

Film shows

Though they hardly come within the scope of a guide to instant home entertainment like this one, it is worth noting that an ever increasing band of home-movie enthusiasts are making their own short feature films. With members of the family as the stars and with the neighbourhood as the location, these amateur film directors are turning out fifteen-minute epics for home consumption and thoroughly enjoying themselves in the process. It is an expensive hobby and the films may well be more fun to make than to watch, but it does make a change from the run-of-the-mill holiday scenes most home-movie makers go in for.

In the age of colour television and stereophonic radio, nobody is interested in old-fashioned peep shows and magic lantern slides, but if you want to impress your friends, but have neither made your own feature film nor own the projector for showing it, you can now hire both. Screens and projectors can be hired for only a few pounds and you can have a feature film for a whole evening for as little as £5. Well-known films cost more (some of them much, much more), but the cinema-in-your-own-home isn't a luxury that needs to be confined to the very rich. If you want to find out more, look up 'film distributors' and 'film projector hire' in your local Yellow Pages and contact the companies in your area that specialise in providing this kind of entertainment.

Ventriloquism

If you plan to take ventriloquism seriously and hope to rival the professionals, then you will have to be prepared to take the necessary time and trouble — and be ready to give a lot of both. Douglas Houldon's book *Ventriloquism for Beginners* (1958), provides an admirable introduction to the art for anyone eager enough to go into it thoroughly. For the less hard-working entertainer, the one who wants to have a bit of fun but does not want to spend much time studying and rehearsing, *perfect* ventriloquism is an impossibility. All the same, you can get very near to the real thing by simply talking without moving your lips!

It isn't easy, but it can be done — with practice. And if you remember these four rules it shouldn't take you long to produce a passable ventriloquial act:

1. Always rehearse in front of a mirror.
2. Always look at your dummy when it's talking and out to the audience when you are.
3. Begin your act with the dummy hidden in a box. To make the dummy's voice sound muffled, roll your tongue up into the roof of your mouth. Then, when you bring the dummy out of the box, bring your tongue back to its usual position. The change in tone of the dummy's voice will add conviction to the performance and draw the audience's attention away from you towards the dummy.
4. Don't try to articulate the consonant sounds too clearly. The attempt will make your lips move. If necessary, tell the audience the dummy is drunk: this explains away his slurred speech and adds to the little fellow's personality.

Of course, the more convincing your dummy, the more readily your audience will accept that it is *him* speaking and not you. It is vital that you give the dummy a definite personality, with attitudes, eccentricities and catchphrases all his own. Dummies can be bought from toy and magic shops for little more than a pound, but if you decide to invent your own, it's a good idea to think of a truly original personality for him. The dummy does not need to be a human being, nor even an animal. You could create a dummy out of an enormous paper flower and explain to the audience that you picked it up from Lewis Carroll's 'Garden of Live Flowers' in *Alice Through the Looking Glass*. If the dummy is sufficiently ingenious, the audience will be more interested in watching and listening to it, than in studying your face and hoping to catch you with your lips moving.

Naturally, the dialogue between you and your dummy will depend on the dummy's personality and your own particular style, but as an exercise you might like to practise with the script that follows. It was used by one of America's most successful ventriloquists in the early years of this century and is useful because it includes some of the most difficult, as well as several of the easiest words and turns of phrase for the ventriloquist. In this case, the ventriloquist is holding two dolls—which will be an even greater distraction to the audience—and their names are Dora and Dan:

PERFORMER: Well, Dora, how are you tonight?
DORA: Terrible!
PERFORMER: Why?
DORA: I was out in the rain and I've caught a frightful cold.
PERFORMER: That's too bad.
DAN: Say funny-face!
PERFORMER: What is it Danny?
DAN: What good does the rain do anyway?
PERFORMER: Well, it helps bring things up out of the ground.
DAN: Oh dear, I hope it won't bring my old woman up.
PERFORMER: You're not married.
DAN: I certainly was married once.
PERFORMER: Only once?
DAN: God knows that's enough for any sane man!
PERFORMER: But you're nothing but a boy.
DAN: I'm older than I look.
PERFORMER: How old are you?
DAN: Over twenty.
PERFORMER: I don't believe it.
DAN: Was you there?
PERFORMER: No, I wasn't.
DAN: Well, I was.

PERFORMER: Dora, I think it's about time we heard from you. Sing us a song, will you?

DORA: I can't sing.

DAN: And for God's sake don't let her try!

PERFORMER: Go on, Dora.

DAN: Don't Dora!

DORA *(singing)*: 'Father, dear father —

DAN *(aside)*: What did I tell you?

DORA *(singing)*: 'Come home with me now,
                    The clock in the steeple strikes one—

DAN: You liar! It's just struck ten.

PERFORMER: Enough of that young man. Since you're so clever, tell me: How much is two times ten?

DAN: It's a good deal.

DORA: It's twenty.

DAN: I knowed that all the time, smartie pants.

PERFORMER: Don't be rude! Let's see if your spelling's as good as your mathematics. How do you spell Constantinople?

DAN: Can't stand what?

DORA: Constantinople.

DAN: Really, Dora? I thought you liked Granny Smith's.

PERFORMER: What are you talking about?

DAN: Dora says she can't stand apples, but I happen to know she's very fond of Granny Smith's.

PERFORMER: She said Constantinople.

DAN: Exactly.

PERFORMER: You're hopeless. I am disgusted with you.

DORA: So am I.

DAN: And do you know what?

PERFORMER: What?

DAN: So am I. For God's sake put me in the box!

If dialogue like that defeats you, but the idea of ventriloquism still appeals, you can always try what's known as 'mute venting'. Rod Hull has been doing it for years with a rapacious emu called Emu. The idea is that you do all the talking and the dummy stays mum, but his *personality* is so strong that he manages to steal the show.

10. MAGIC

Each of the twenty tricks that follow can be mastered in under a minute. Practice, of course, will make perfect, but the idea is to provide you with some ready-made magic, requiring little real wizardry but plenty of fun. If you want to work at the magician's craft and see yourself as a potential member of the Magic Circle, consult Joseph Dunninger's *Complete Encyclopedia of Magic* (1970). If not, read on.

The banana trick

The effect: You produce an ordinary banana and explain to the members of the audience that, thanks to your magic powers, you can cut it up before unzipping it. You then pronounce the magic words and invite one of your audience to unpeel the banana. As they do so, it falls into three separate pieces.

The explanation: You must tamper with the banana before performing the trick. All you need is a long thin needle and all you have to do is insert it at two points down one of the seams of the banana skin and move the needle gently from side to side. When you come to unzip the banana, it will appear to have been cut by a knife at both points. The pin-holes will be unnoticeable.

If you want to add conviction to the trick, tamper with *all* the bananas in the bunch and invite a member of the audience to choose any one.

Burning tissue

The effect: You show your audience that your hands are perfectly empty and that you have nothing up your sleeves except your arms. You then take a piece of colourful tissue paper, about a foot square, and light it with a match. You watch it burn away and just as it's about to be burnt to a cinder you wave your hand and—hey presto!—the piece of tissue paper is restored.

The explanation: Your hands are indeed empty when you start the trick, but by the time you have lit the piece of tissue paper you have a substitute in your hand ready and waiting to amaze the audience. Before beginning the performance you have hidden the substitute tissue in the matchbox which is used during the trick. The matchbox is lying on the table half-open and you have concealed the tissue in the space vacated by the tray of matches which is pushed half way out. When you pick up the matchbox to light the original tissue you are careful to keep the end containing the tissue away from the audience and having extracted the match you need, the act of closing the matchbox will force the substitute tissue into the palm of your hand.

The coin in hand trick

The effect: Give a member of the audience a coin, turn your back and ask him to hold the fist that is carrying the coin to their forehead. Then get them to hold out both clenched fists, turn round and tell them in which hand the coin is hidden.

The explanation: The hand that carried the coin and was held to the forehead will be *paler* than the other hand when the clenched fists are presented.

Fiery hand

The effect: You produce several sheets of drawing paper and tell the audience you are going to write something rather special on the paper. You then look for your pen, but cannot find it. In desperation you ask a member of the audience who happens to be smoking if you can borrow his cigarette. Taking it, you simply touch the paper with it and, lo and behold, your message appears in letters of fire.

The explanation: You have written the message on the paper earlier in an invisible ink that was a solution of nitrate of potash. Providing you didn't lift pen from paper, once you have ignited the dried solution with the cigarette it will burn its way right through the message.

The hidden coin

The effect: You place three plates on the table and invite members of the audience to hide a coin under one of the plates while you are out of the room. They do so and, on your return, without touching any of the plates you are able to tell them exactly where the coin is hidden.

The explanation: You have a confederate — and he must be a smoker. If the coin is under the centre plate, he holds his cigarette in the middle of his mouth; if it's under the left plate, he holds it in the left of his mouth; if it's under the right plate, he holds it in the right of his mouth. If the members of the audience have tried to be clever and haven't hidden the coin under any of the plates at all, the confederate takes his cigarette right out of his mouth!

Inflammable sugar

The effect: You challenge a member of the audience to light an ordinary sugar lump with an ordinary match. They pick a lump from the sugar bowl and try. They fail. You pick out another lump and succeed.

The explanation: If you have rubbed one side of the lump of sugar with cigarette ash, it will light with ease, and the ash, acting as a kind of wick, will mean that the sugar lump will go on burning for quite a time.

Initial magic

The effect: You invite a member of the audience to write his initials in ink on the side of a sugar lump. You then drop the sugar lump into a beaker of water, place the member of the audience's hand over the beaker and a moment later remove his hand to reveal to him that his initials have disappeared from the sugar lump and are now imprinted on the palm of his hand.

The explanation: You must begin the trick with a damp thumb. Once he has written his initials on the sugar, press your thumb against the initials (so transferring them on to your thumb) and then, as you are showing him how to hold his hand over the beaker, press your thumb against his palm — so transferring the initials there.

The Kellar string and straw trick

The effect: Devised by Kellar, the great American magician, this trick is as ingenious as it is simple. You thread a piece of string through a drinking straw, then bend the straw in half and, with a pair of scissors, cut the straw into two. The pieces of straw are then straightened out and the string is pulled away still in one piece.

The explanation: Before performing the trick you have made a razor cut of about two inches in the middle of the straw, so that when the straw is bent, with the cut on the inside, the string, if the ends are pulled, will come clear of the bend. The exposed fragment of string you conceal with your thumb and forefinger as you cut the straw with the scissors. Finally you hold the pieces of straw in your closed left hand while you extract the intact string with your right.

The magic loop

The effect: You take a strip of paper, three feet long and an inch wide. You join the ends together and tell your audience that by simply cutting a line down the centre of the paper, you will turn the one large loop into two smaller ones.

The explanation: As you join the ends together to make the large loop you twist one end round twice.

Match magic

The effect: You invite a member of the audience to lend you a match, having first marked the match so that there will be no jiggery-pokery in the course of the trick. You are given the marked match and place it in the centre of a large handkerchief. Folding one end of the handkerchief over the match and then the other, you now invite members of the audience to feel that the match is there and then break it. Get several different people to break it in different places. When they have done so, open up the handkerchief and reveal the original match complete in one piece.

The explanation: Before beginning the trick you will have concealed a second match in the *seam* of the handkerchief. As you fold the handkerchief, you make sure that the match the members of the audience feel and break is the concealed one. The moment the trick is over and while the audience is examining the unharmed matchstick, slip the handkerchief into your pocket and produce a substitute handkerchief (with nothing hidden in its seams) just in case anyone should want to examine it.

Mind reading

The effect: You invite members of the audience to write down brief phrases, sentences or thoughts on slips of paper provided by you. The slips are then folded so that the writing is hidden and placed in a hat. You now proceed to pick out one of the slips and, without looking at it, hold it to your forehead and reveal to the audience what the wording on the piece of paper is. You repeat this miracle with all the slips of paper and gratefully acknowledge the thunderous applause.

The explanation: Inside the hat you have already planted a slip of paper with your own phrase on it. You've tucked it into the lining where you can get at it when you want it, which is when you are about to reveal your *final* phrase. You begin by picking out any one of the audience's slips and by holding it to your forehead. You then say that the phrase written is the one you have in fact written on your hidden slip. Once you've said it, you open the slip apparently to check and in fact read what your next phrase is going to be. You pick out a new slip, hold it to your forehead, announce the phrase you read on the previous slip, wait for the gasp of recognition from the member of the audience concerned and carry on.

Money from nowhere

The effect: You show the audience your empty hands, pull up your sleeves to reveal that you've nothing hidden and then — out of the blue — produce a neatly folded £1 note.

The explanation: The note is concealed in the folds of your jacket (or jersey or shirt or blouse) on top of the left elbow joint. It doesn't fall out of its place of concealment because you hold your arms upward when revealing that your hands are empty. When you pull up your sleeves you extract the note as you are pulling up the left sleeve.

The object vanishes

The effect: Holding a small object in your left hand, you cover it with a magic handkerchief. You then invite several members of the audience to feel your hand to make sure the object is still there. You then whisk away the handkerchief and reveal a completely empty hand.

The explanation: You have a confederate. He is the last member of the audience to whom you offer your hand and, as he feels it, he *removes* the hidden object.

Odds and evens

The effect: You are blindfolded and invite a member of the audience to hold an odd number of coins in one hand and an even number in the other. Then ask him to multiply the number of coins in his right hand by any even number and to multiply the number of coins in his left hand by any uneven number and to add the two answers together. He then gives you the final figure and you tell him which hand is holding the even number of coins and which the odd number.

The explanation: If the total number he gives you after he has done the sum is *odd*, the number of coins in his right hand is *even*, and vice-versa.

Rattle 'em

The effect: You put a coin in one of three matchboxes, shuffle the boxes about and lay them on the table. Pick up one box and rattle it to show the audience where the coin is and shuffle the three boxes again. Now invite a member of the audience to find the box containing the coin. He'll fail.

The explanation: You keep a fourth box up your sleeve and it too contains a coin, so when you pick up the box and rattle it to show the audience where the coin is the box you are holding is in fact empty and the rattle they can hear comes from the hidden box up your sleeve.

Rubber pencil

The effect: You borrow an ordinary pencil from a member of the audience and, with much muttering of 'Hocus-pocus' and 'Abracadabra', you wave it in the air, and it appears to turn into a rubber pencil.

The explanation: This is simply an optical illusion. If you hold the pencil between the first finger and thumb about an inch from the end and gently move your hand up and down while holding the pencil quite loosely, the pencil will look as if it is bending.

Secrets of the age

The effect: You explain to your audience that with the aid of this simple chart you will reveal to any member of the audience under the age of sixty-four exactly how old they are. (Those who are sixty-four or more are spared the embarrassment of having their date of birth revealed).

1	2	4	8	16	32
3	3	5	9	17	33
5	6	6	10	18	34
7	7	7	11	19	35
9	10	12	12	20	36
11	11	13	13	21	37
13	14	14	14	22	38
15	15	15	15	23	39
17	18	20	24	24	40
19	19	21	25	25	41
21	22	22	26	26	42
23	23	23	27	27	43
25	26	28	28	28	44
27	27	29	29	29	45
29	30	30	30	30	46
31	31	31	31	31	47
33	34	36	40	48	48
35	35	37	41	49	49
37	38	38	42	50	50
39	39	39	43	51	51
41	42	44	44	52	52
43	43	45	45	53	53
45	46	46	46	54	54
47	47	47	47	55	55
49	50	52	56	56	56
51	51	53	57	57	57
53	54	54	58	58	58
55	55	55	59	59	59
57	58	60	60	60	60
59	59	61	61	61	61
61	62	62	62	62	62
63	63	63	63	63	63

Invite any member of the audience to tell you in which column or columns their age appears. When they have done so, simply tell them how old they are.

The explanation: Whatever column or columns a person tells you contains his or her age you add up the numbers at the top of those columns and the total gives you the answer. For example, 18 appears in the second and the fifth columns and the figures at the top of these columns are 2 and 16, which adds up to 18.

Telepathy

The effect: You invite the members of your audience to agree on an object while you are out of the room. On your return one of the audience asks you what the mystery object is, giving you a list to choose from, and the moment he mentions the object in question you say 'That's it'.

The explanation: You have a confederate and he is the member of the audience who suggests the objects to you. Just before mentioning the object itself, he will mention another object that has four legs. For example, were the mystery object the television set, he would begin like this: 'Is it the clock? Is it the painting? Is it me? Is it the fireplace? Is it the doorknob? Is it the table? Is it the television set?' 'Yes, that's it' you say confidently, knowing it must be because it was the first item mentioned after an object with four legs.

The vanishing coin

The effect: A coin is folded inside a piece of paper; the paper is then torn up; the coin has vanished!

The explanation: The piece of paper should be about four inches square and the coin should be placed in the middle of the paper about an inch and a half from the lower edge. The paper below the coin is folded upwards, so concealing it, the top of the paper is folded to the back and, finally, the sides of the paper are also folded back. If this is done swiftly and smartly, it will appear that the coin is securely folded inside the paper. In fact there is one open side from which the coin can slide secretly into your hand, where you conceal it while tearing the paper. When you pass the torn bits of paper to the audience for inspection, you can use the distraction to slip the coin from your hand to your pocket.

Vanishing gloves

The effect: This is an elementary but engaging trick with which to begin your act. You appear, wearing an elegant pair of white magician's gloves, you remove them quite casually and they disappear!

The explanation: The palm of each glove has elastic attached to it and the other end of the elastic is pinned inside your coat sleeves. When the gloves are removed they automatically shoot up your sleeves, thus creating the illusion. This is not a trick to build up: it's just a little piece of business that sets the scene for the magic to follow.

11. FORTUNE-TELLING

Methods of fortune-telling are many and some are splendid. The ones described in this chapter are particularly suitable for home entertainment, but for those who want more than amusement — for those who want their fortunes very definitely foretold — the place to visit is 'Zodiac: the Astrological Emporium' at 3 Kensington Mall, London W8, where more detailed information on astrology, palmistry, phrenology and tea-cup divining is readily available.

Astrology

Knowing the year, day, hour and moment of your birth, a serious astrologer could, having done some considerable homework, provide you with something resembling a portrait of your inner self and an outline of the possibilities that lie ahead. The homework would be considerable because the science of astrology involves much more than a nodding acquaintance with the signs of the zodiac. To begin with, the position of the planets at the moment of birth has to be calculated — and that takes time. And time is something the home entertainer is unlikely to have to spare. The serious student of astrology should equip himself with a copy of Derek and Julia Parker's tome, *The Compleat Astrologer*. It will tell him all he needs to know, though however seriously he takes his astrology he should never forget the age-old motto: the stars incline, they do not compel.

All the home entertainer can hope to do is fool about in the shallows and the most enjoyable way of doing just that is to enquire of his friends their dates of birth and analyse their personalties (and hence the potential of their lives). Each of the twelve signs of the zodiac is indicative of certain traits and the home entertainer can *either* tell a subject what his virtues and limitations are having discovered his particular sign, *or* guess the sign having observed the subject's characteristics. Either way, since people love nothing so much as hearing about themselves, this form of simplified astrology will afford enormous pleasure.

These are the twelve signs and the traits particularly associated with them:

AQUARIUS: *20th January to 19th February*
independent, warm, willing, enthusiastic, progressive, faithful, idealistic, unpredictable, obstinate, original, unconventional.
Colour: blue.

PISCES: *20th February to 21st March*
emotional, caring, kind, sensitive, flexible, vague, unpractical, theatrical, artistic, indecisive.
Colour: sea-green.

ARIES: *22nd March to 22nd April*
courageous, adventurous, energetic, direct, impatient, selfish, quick-witted, quick-tempered, eager, questing, questioning.
Colour: red.

TAURUS: *21st April to 21st May*
positive, practical, reliable, solid, secure, dogmatic, self-willed, persistent, obstinate, sure-footed, trustworthy, greedy, unoriginal.
Colours: pink and pale blue.

GEMINI: *22nd May to 22nd June*
clever, witty, intelligent, lively, talkative, versatile, progressive, restless, inquisitive, gossipy, superficial, secretive, cunning.
Colour: yellow.

CANCER: *23rd June to 23rd July*
generous, kindly, thoughtful, protective, conservative, shrewd, home-loving, over-emotional, over-sensitive, weak, emotionally self-indulgent.
Colours: grey and green.

LEO: *24th July to 23rd August*
generous, big-hearted, enthusiastic, domineering, dramatic, arrogant, power-conscious, class-conscious, egotistical, pedantic.
Colour: orange.

VIRGO: *24th August to 23rd September*
chaste, modest, retiring, neat, precise, fastidious, fussy, conventional, tense, hard-working, apparently unemotional.
Colours: navy blue and brown.

LIBRA: *24th September to 23rd October*
optimistic, idealistic, enthusiastic, romantic, liberal, cultured, frivolous, easily influenced, self-indulgent.
Colours: pink and pale blue.

SCORPIO: *24th October to 22nd November*
sex-orientated, lusty, emotional, imaginative, eager, determined, obstinate, jealous, secretive, conspiratorial.
Colour: dark red.

SAGITTARIUS: *23rd November to 22nd December*
carefree, optimistic, flexible, freedom-loving, honest, reliable, thorough, restless, careless, irresponsible, over-enthusiastic.
Colour: purple.

CAPRICORN: *23rd December to 19th January*
ambitious, careful, cautious, patient, disciplined, determined, pessimistic, avaricious, shy, industrious, self-absorbed, self-sufficient.
Colour: black.

Cards

'Reading the cards' is one of the oldest ways of telling fortunes and requires a complete familiarity with their meanings on the part of the card interpreter. By tradition these are the characteristics and events indicated by the fifty-two cards in the pack:

Clubs

Ace: wealth and prosperity.
King: upright, affectionate.
Queen: deeply in love.
Knave: generous and sincere.
10: an unexpected fortune.
 9: obstinacy and a dispute with friends.
 8: a love of money.
 7: fortune and great happiness.
 6: a lucrative partnership.
 5: marriage to a wealthy person.
 4: inconstancy.
 3: a second or third marriage.
 2: opposition.

Hearts

Ace: pleasure, but when with spades quarrelling, when with diamonds absent friends, when with clubs festivities.
King: passion.
Queen: affectionate.
Knave: the subject's dearest friend.
10: the antidote to any bad cards lying near it and the card that confirms the good things.
 9: wealth and a wish.
 8: feasting and merry-making.
 7: infidelity.
 6: generosity.
 5: uncertainty.
 4: marriage late in life.
 3: imprudence.
 2: great success and good fortune.

Spades

Ace: a love affair or, if upside-down, a death.
King: an ambitious person.
Queen: a treacherous friend.
Knave: indolence.
10: bad luck.
 9: terrible luck (this is the worst card in the pack).
 8: opposition from friends.
 7: sorrow.
 6: great fortune.
 5: success and a happy marriage.
 4: illness or a small loss of money.
 3: an unfortunate marriage.
 2: a death.

Diamonds

Ace: a letter, the nature of which will be indicated by the card that lies next to it.
King: hot temper.
Queen: flirtatious.
Knave: selfishness.
10: money.
 9: a traveller.
 8: marriage late in life.
 7: a gambler.
 6: early marriage.
 5: friendship.
 4: unhappy marriage.
 3: quarrels, law-suits, disagreements.
 2: a serious love affair.

Having mastered the meaning of the cards, the interpreter is ready for his first subject. He invites the subject to shuffle the cards thoroughly and cut them into three packs, all face upwards. The three packs give an overall picture. (For example the Nine of Hearts, followed by the Ace of Spades, followed by the Four of Diamonds, would indicate a wish about a love-affair leading to an unhappy marriage, while the Ace of Diamonds followed by the Queen of Spades followed by the Seven of Spades would indicate the imminent arrival of a letter from a treacherous friend bringing sad news.)

For a more detailed interpretation, gather the three packs together again and, without shuffling the cards, deal them into seven piles. The top card on each pile is the one to interpret and each particular pile affects a different area of the subject's life:

Pile 1 relates to the subject's inner self.
Pile 2 relates to the subject's house and home-life.
Pile 3 relates to the subject's wishes.
Pile 4 relates to what the subject expects will happen to him.
Pile 5 relates to what the subject does *not* expect.
Pile 6 relates to what is sure to come true.
Pile 7 relates to the events of that very day.

The golden rule for card interpreters is: never attemps to read the cards for the same subject twice. It will only confuse you, them and the cards.

Cup divining

The art of interpreting tea-leaves has suffered a severe set-back since the universal acceptance of tea-bags. Nowadays, very few people find dregs at the bottom of their tea-cups, which means that they are losing a valuable opportunity, for the tea-leaves — or the grains of coffee — that lurk in a cup after it has been drunk reveal much about the future fortune of the individual whose cup it is.

Before listing some of the more common symbols that turn up inside tea-cups, it is important to point out a few general rules:

1. The handle of the cup indicates house and home and the nearness of the leaves to the brim of the cup suggests how near or far the future incidents that are foretold are likely to take place.
2. Leaves near the brim of the cup suggest that the forthcoming events will be fairly immediate.
3. Leaves at the bottom of the cup generally bode ill.
4. Leaves to the left of the handle are indicative of opportunities missed and on the right of possibilities still to come.
5. Unless the tea or coffee has actually been drunk by the subject, the pattern of the leaves will be meaningless.

When the cup is drained, the interpreter will be able to see that the leaves form one or more different patterns and this is what some of those patterns indicate can be expected during the life of the person who has been drinking from the cup:

Animals:

   bear: wild schemes and foreign travel

   cat: treachery

   cow: great wealth

   dog: the fidelity of friends

   donkey: a contented life

   horse: a lover

   lamb: pleasures to come

   lion: friends in high places

   mouse: poverty and ill-fortune

   wolf: greed

   zebra: a foreign lover

Arrow: bad news

Basket: a gift

Bees: industry and common sense

Bell: forthcoming marriage

Birds:

   canary: a new lover

   chicken: a well-ordered life

   dove: harmony

   duck: new riches

   eagle: fame and fortune

   owl: bad news

   parrot: a scandal just ahead

   peacock: a vain nature

   swan: a lover who will bring happiness

   vulture: cruelty, infidelity and great unhappiness

Boat: discovery

Book: self-fulfilment

Butterfly: frivolity and happiness

Clock: death

Clouds: oncoming problems

Coffin: a long but not necessarily fatal illness

Cross: suffering to come

Crown: success

Drum: war and argument

Egg: good fortune

Eye: keen observation

Fish: financial gains

Flowers: love, happiness, good will

Fruit: general good fortune

Grapes: a successful love affair
Gun: a slanderous attack
Harp: a romance
Hat: a new rival
Key: newly found prosperity
Ladder: progress in professional life
Man: a visitor who is unexpected
Mermaid: evil temptation to be faced
Moon: a sad or even tragic love affair
Mountain: a possibly hazardous journey ahead
Mushroom: respite and rest in the near future
Necklace: conquest
Ring: an unexpected marriage
Scissors: unexpected separation

Ship: discovery of wealth
Spider: subterfuge
Star: hope for the future
Spoon: general good fortune
Tortoise: the promise of triumph over adversity
Tree: good fortune in the years ahead
Umbrella: protection in adversity
Wheel: advancement whatever the odds
Windmill: hard work ahead
Wings: news, neither good nor bad
Woman: wealth (in the case of a woman) or the possibility of marrying a widow (in the case of a man)

Dice

Draw a magic circle on the table. Now throw three dice from a cup into the magic circle. If any of the dice falls outside the circle, ignore it . Add up the numbers of the dice inside the circle and find out what the future holds in store for you. This is what the different totals signify:

  1: predicting catastrophe
  2: you will soon lose your job
  3: an accident awaits you
  4: a rise in your position
  5: you will soon meet a close friend
  6: predicting loss of some kind
  7: predicting a scandal
  8: predicting a reproach that you deserve
  9: predicting a wedding
 10: predicting a christening
 11: predicting trouble for the one you love

12: predicting the arrival of an important letter
13: predicting tears
14: warning you to beware of an enemy
15: predicting good fortune and happiness
16: predicting a journey
17: predicting a journey across water
18: success in business will come to you and all your wishes should come true

Graphology

Graphology is the science of interpreting handwriting. To master the skill requires months of practice, but a superficial understanding of a person's character can be gained from even the most casual acquaintance with their style of handwriting. The home entertainer won't want to furnish his subject with a full character analysis, but will want to come up with a few insights to impress the subject and amuse the rest of the company.

For this purpose there are seven letters which reveal a great deal very quickly. They are A, B, C, D, E, M and T and the home graphologist should study them carefully for the secrets they hold. This, in essence, is what each of them can show:

A: A well-made, simple *A* indicates refinement, gentleness, intelligence, perhaps even poetic feelings. Flourishes are an unhealthy sign, indicating in the *A* pretension and egotism. If the small *a* is not properly joined up, this suggests a gossipy nature. (The same is true of an incomplete *o.)*

B: A simple, clear-cut *B* indicates reticence and discretion. An extravagant, broad *B* suggests ostentation and arrogance. A well-rounded, rather loopy *b* is indicative of an affectionate nature.

C: A well-rounded capital *C* suggests an indolent but well-meaning and good-humoured nature. But a *C,* large or small, with a curly tail suggests selfishness.

D: The small *d* flowing into the letter next to it suggests a logical mind and a well-balanced disposition. An over-elaborate *D,* whether large or small, suggests an ill-balanced nature and the possibility of emotional instability.

E: A firm, large capital *E* indicates an egotistical temperament, most especially when the tail curls up. A long tail in a small *e* suggests a vivid imagination and an even temper. An exaggerated tail to the *e* reveals a careless, thoughtless nature.

M: The first high loop in the *M* is indicative of ambition, a small start to the letter indicating lack of ambition, and a big, bold start suggesting great ambition. An elaborate final flourish to the *M* reveals a self-centred personality, while a moderate one suggests strength of will and force of character.

T: The significance with the letter *T* lies in the way in which it is crossed. A thickly crossed *T*, large or small, indicates energy; a flick of the pen rather than a separate crossing of the *T* suggests perseverance; an abrupt little crossing to the *T* suggests short temper; and a *t* crossed high indicates an impulsive nature.

The graphologist seeking quick insights through a brief look at a sample of someone's handwriting should also remember that wide spacing between lines suggests extravagance and when accompanied by rounded terminal flourishes to the letters, great good nature and generosity. Tightly spaced lines and very precise abrupt handwriting suggest a more introverted, humourless and self-seeking personality.

Occult

It is believed by many that there are in this world forces, powers, influences, spirits (call them what you will) that we do not fully comprehend, but with which we can make contact. There are all sorts of ways to attempt to 'summon up the supernatural' or 'get in touch with the other side', but the home entertainer hoping to communicate with the other worlds would be well advised to begin with fairly simple methods.

Table tapping is a good one. This involves everyone in the group sitting around a table (preferably a round one) with their fingers gently resting on the surface of the table. The leader then sets the scene by explaining that he wants to call the other side and asks, 'Is anyone there?' If he is very lucky and the concentration of the group is absolute he may get a reply. The replies come in the form of taps from the table. If the table bumps up and down once the answer is 'Yes', if twice the answer is 'No'. Having established contact with the spirit of the other side the leader asks for a specific individual and, if that individual is available and willing to communicate, some sort of dialogue can be established. It is imperative that the fingers are laid as lightly as possible on the table and that the knees of those sitting round the table remain absolutely still so that there can be no question of the group being taken for a ride by one of its members.

If you would like more explicit information than that which the 'Yes' and 'No' system affords, the roving glass is worth trying. Again the group sit round a circular table. This time however, they lay their index fingers lightly on the rim of an upturned glass. Around the table are letters of the alphabet printed on cards, so that when a question has been put to whoever happens to be on the other side they can give their reply or message (or warning or protest or whatever) by spelling it out, leading the glass from one letter to the next. Again it is imperative that none of the group is tempted to exert any pressure on the glass.

If you are still unsatisfied having extracted yesses and noes and whole sentences from the other side, you can always have a go at getting a *spoken* reply. To do this you simply need a tape recorder and a brand-new tape. Ask your questions, put the recorder on to record, wait a moment or two and play back whatever has been recorded. It may take a long while to discern the voice or voices on the tape, but there are those who maintain it can be done. Indeed, for a detailed description of experiments involving electronic communication with the dead consult Konstantin Raudive's *Breakthrough* (1971) and for practical details as to how it's done read Peter Bander's *Carry On Talking* (1972). And if you want to hear what these voices sound like, a record (apparently including the voice of the late Sir Winston Churchill among others) can be obtained from Vista Records, 64a Lansdown Road, London W11 2LR.

Palmistry

No two hands are alike and the successful palmist is the one who studies the hand as a whole and realises that the fingers can reveal as much as the palm.

In palmist's jargon, the first finger is called Jupiter, the second Saturn, the third Apollo, the fourth Mercury and the thumb is known as Pollux. The size , shape and spacing of the fingers all have their special meanings. A wide space between Jupiter and Saturn shows originality of thought and outlook. And when the Jupiter finger is upright and straight and not abnormally long, that signifies a just but candid nature. If the finger is longer than the others it suggests a desire to dominate. If it's shorter, it indicates a weakness of character and an inability to take responsibilities. A short Jupiter reveals an unenthusiastic person, a long one a sympathetic and tactful person, a square one an honest but almost over-frank person.

A broad Saturn finger shows gravity and depth of character. A short Saturn suggests an imprudent, impulsive personality. A square Saturn is indicative of a clear head and a cool approach to life.

The Apollo finger is the one that reveals the owner's artistic tendencies. If the finger is unusually long and forward, painting, drawing and sculpture are the important arts. If it is pointed, it means that the owner is far more an artist than anything else. If the finger is flat and square, the owner is an individual with a marvellous sense of form and colour.

The Mercury finger is there to indicate the setbacks that may beset the owner of the hand in question. A pointed Mercury shows an ability to cope with life's problems, with an instinct for survival and a sense of proper discrimination. A square Mercury suggests a love of science and a sound reasoning ability, but a short Mercury, particularly one set lower than the other fingers, reveals that the owner will have to come to terms with more difficulties than most.

Beneath each finger rest their respective mounts. There are two mounts of Mars: one at the base of the Jupiter mount and the other at the base of the Mercury mount. The mount of Luna is directly opposite the mount of Venus, which is found where the thumb joins the wrist. These mounts and their proximity to one another are important and the true palmist will feel and study them carefully.

Jupiter approaching Saturn indicates timidity and self-consciousness. Saturn approaching Apollo indicates a melancholic spirit. Apollo approaching Mercury indicates humanity and even temper. Mercury approaching Mars indicates self-reliance and an ability to cope with fear and danger. Mars approaching Mercury indicates originality. Luna approaching the wrist indicates a frivolous, pleasure-seeking nature.

As the palmist feels the hand, he will notice which of the mounts are most prominent and can draw significant conclusions. Since Jupiter and Mercury reveal worldly, versatile traits, Jupiter and Apollo worthy and noble traits, Jupiter and Venus selfish and vain traits, Saturn and Mercury weak traits, hands where these particular mounts are prominent usually belong to shallow, unhappy people who find concentration and work difficult.

This is what the prominence of other mounts traditionally indicates: Saturn and Mars — a thrifty, almost avaricious nature; Saturn and Luna — self-mistrust and a tendency towards depression; Apollo and Luna — great imagination; Apollo and Mars — great creativity and a love of danger; Mercury and Mars — buoyant, good humoured personality; Mercury and Venus — a cynical temperament; Venus and Apollo — generosity of spirit; Mercury and Luna — a highly developed sense of fun.

Of course, while the shape of the fingers and the bumps on the palm are crucial, the lines on the palm must not be neglected. There are seven major lines on which to concentrate and each of them reveals a different aspect of the personality:

1. The life line, which forms a semi-circle at the base of the thumb;
2. The head line which traverses the palm and forms an angle with the life line;
3. The heart line which runs above and parallel with the head line;
4. The fate line which runs vertically from mount Saturn to the wrist;
5. The fortune line which runs parallel with the fate line from mount Apollo to mount Luna;
6. The line of health which forms an angle with the base of the life line and reaches almost to mount Mercury;
7. The line of intuition, which curves from mount Mercury to mount Luna.

The appearance along any of these lines of breaks in the line, stars, crosses, dots, suggests misfortune, unhappiness and danger in the area indicated by the line. Triangles, squares and circles on the mounts indicate good fortune and happiness.

The palmist must obviously interpret what he sees with all the intuition and sensitivity he can muster. He must also remember that the two hands go together and never make the mistake of agreeing to tell the fortune of a one-armed man. The left hand indicates natural tendencies, while the right indicates how far the good and bad propensities of the individual have been developed and it is quite possible that the former can suggest a potential that does not materialise in the latter. For example, a strong clear heart line in the left hand may appear as a broken and shorter heart line in the second, indicating that a potentially happy and fruitful love life has been or will be marred.

Finally, the palmist must never forget the golden rule: from what you see tell nothing but the truth, but do not always tell the whole truth.

Phrenology

The phrenologist can interpret the character and reveal the potential of an individual by feeling his cranium. The cranium is a mass of little bumps and each one has a special meaning. The phrenologist must feel a whole range of heads before he can tell what is a normal protuberance and what is too prominent or too small. Of course, if Yul Brynner is a friend, you can use him as your guinea-pig. If he isn't, anyone will do providing you can get your fingers through their hair and really feel every part of the cranium.

These are the thirty-two different parts:

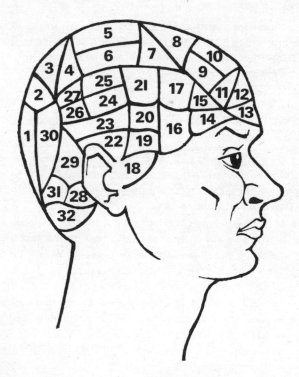

The thirty-two parts of the cranium

And this is what they mean:

1. *Amativeness*. Normal: interest in the opposite sex. Too prominent: interested only in material things. Too small: coldness, indifference.
2. *Conjugal affection*. Normal: constancy, fidelity. Too prominent: jealousy and selfishness. Too small: infidelity, adultery.
3. *Parental love*. Normal: selfish love of children. Too prominent: monopolising affection. Too small: cold, heartless.
4. *Friendship*. Normal: sociable, warm. Too prominent: over-demanding. Too small: inability to make friends.
5. *Inhabitiveness*. Normal: love of home. Too prominent: intense dislike of travel. Too small: restless urge to travel.
6. *Continuity*. Normal: ability to concentrate. Too prominent: one-track mind. Too small: inability to concentrate.
7. *Vitativeness*. Normal: joy for living. Too prominent: morbid. Too small: lack of interest in life.
8. *Combativeness*. Normal: courageous. Too prominent: quarrelsome. Too small: cowardly.
9. *Destructiveness*. Normal: tough, consistent. Too prominent: vindictive. Too small: weakness.
10. *Alimentiveness*. Normal: healthy appetite. Too prominent: gluttonous. Too small: lack of appetite.
11. *Secretiveness*. Normal: tactful. Too prominent: deceitfulness. Too small: lack of discretion.
12. *Cautiousness*. Normal: prudence. Too prominent: timidity. Too small: recklessness.
13. *Approbativeness*. Normal: good breeding and manners. Too prominent: ostentatious. Too small: unconventional and ill-mannered.
14. *Self-esteem*. Normal: sense of individuality. Too prominent: conceit. Too small: sense of incompetence.
14. *Conscientiousness*. Normal: high regard for duty. Too prominent: hyper-sensitive. Too small: lacking in principle.
15. *Hope*. Normal: optimistic. Too prominent: foolhardy. Too small: melancholic.
16. *Spirituality*. Normal: reverential. Too prominent: fanatical. Too small: cynical.
17. *Veneration*. Normal: modesty. Too prominent: obsessiveness. Too small: disrespectfulness.

18. *Benevolence:* Normal: generous. Too prominent: over-generous. Too small: mean.
19. *Individuality.* Normal: desire for knowledge. Too prominent: over inquisitive. Too small: no sense of humour.
20. *Form.* Normal: good memory. Too prominent: coldly ordered mind. Too small: poor memory.
21. *Size.* Normal: good ability to judge perspective and proportions. Too prominent: forever making unfair comparisons. Too small: lack of sense of perspective and proportion.
22. *Weight.* Normal: inclined towards mathematics. Too prominent: obsessive interest in the sciences. Too small: lack of mental and physical co-ordination.
23. *Colour.* Normal: delight in nature. Too prominent: hypersensitive to uncongenial environments. Too small: lack of artistic sensibility.
24. *Order.* Normal: ability to plan. Too prominent: fussy. Too small: slovenly.
25. *Calculation.* Normal: the power to sum up situations. Too prominent: self-interest. Too small: financial imprudence.
26. *Locality.* Normal: excellent sense of observation. Too prominent: passion for exploration. Too small: lack of observation.
27. *Eventuality.* Normal: interest in the here and now. Too prominent: interest in trivial matters. Too small: poor memory of recent events.
28. *Time.* Normal: punctuality. Too prominent: obsessive interest in dates, anniversaries, times of appointments. Too small: slackness.
29. *Tune.* Normal: sense of harmony. Too prominent: passion for music. Too small: lack of artistic appreciation.
30. *Language.* Normal: fluent. Too prominent: wordy. Too small: inarticulate.
31. *Causality.* Normal: power of reasoning. Too prominent: theoretical rather than practical in approach. Too small: inability to think for oneself.
32. *Comparison.* Normal: ability to sort fact from fiction. Too prominent: over-critical nature. Too small: credulous, easily fooled.

It must be admitted that most phrenologists have very small Comparison bumps and very large Language ones, but with sensitive fingers and the aid of this guide much can be revealed.

12. HOME ENTERTAINER SUPERSTAR

When you have tried all the forms of home entertainment described in this book, when you've played all the games and solved all the puzzles, when you've sung all the songs and mastered all the tricks, you might, for a change, be eager to try something more ambitious, more daring, more dramatic. If that's the case, then this is your chapter, for it contains the secrets of one of the world's greatest circus and side-show performers, Walter Shaw of Victoria, Missouri, USA. None but the insane, the suicidal or the superhuman will want to try them, but just in case you happen to be one or another of these, or all three, be sure to read the instructions several times before trying any of the tricks. They work (Shaw made a small fortune), they're not lethal (Shaw lived to a grand old age) and once you have mastered them you will certainly become a home entertainer superstar. Good luck!

Fire eating

Burning coals. 'Take burnt cotton on a saucer saturated with alcohol which looks like heated charcoal; when lit, eat with a fork.'

Sealing wax. 'Take a stick of common express wax in one hand and a candle in the other; melt the wax over the candle, and put on your tongue while blazing. The moisture of your mouth cools it almost instantly, care should be taken not to get any on the lips, chin or hands.'

Living gas jet. 'Get the very lightest petrol, take a small sponge and saturate well with the petrol, squeezing the surplus liquor into a saucer. Place the sponge in a handkerchief, step to the front of the stage and wipe your mouth. Secretly place the sponge in your mouth, which you close tightly, and after wiping your mouth or lips again, carefully throw back your head and open your lips a little and blow your breath out slowly. Now by holding a lighted candle or match 6 or 8 inches from your mouth, but directly in front of it, your breath will take fire and make a solid flame from 12 to 15 inches in length and lasting as long as you expel your breath; when ready to shut off, just close your lips tightly and it is out. Remove the sponge under cover of the handkerchief.'

To eat coals of fire out of a furnace. 'In the first place make a good charcoal fire in the furnace. Just before commencing your act throw in three or four pieces of soft pine, which when burnt to a coal cannot be distinguished from charcoal, except by sticking your fork in it. This will not burn you in the least while the genuine charcoal will. You can stick your fork into these coals without any difficulty, but the charcoal is brittle and hard; it breaks before the fork goes into it.'

How to make the solution for fire-eating. 'Take one ounce of powdered alum, one ounce of bicarbonate of soda, one ounce of Castile soap, and one ounce of pure water. Mix together until well dissolved, and add one pint of strong vinegar. Let this stand for forty-eight hours and it is ready for use. Wash the mouth with this preparation until the flesh has become well coated, and you are ready for business. After you have used this solution a short time you will find that you can eat fire as easily as you can chestnuts or pie.'

The human pincushion

'For this act, instead of using pins and needles, you use a fine wire, cut into lengths the size of pins and needles; this wire, being very bright, at a short distance will look like pins and needles. Instead of inserting these pieces of wire into the flesh you merely stick them into your skin, and by cutting some pieces shorter than others it will appear as though some were inserted further than others.

'Then borrow a lady's gold breast-pin and run it through the fleshy part of your arm, and run two needles through each ear and a knitting needle through the calf of your leg. To do this go to your doctor and have him pierce your ears, the fleshy part of your arm and the calf of your leg, just as a lady would get her ears pierced for earrings. Let the doctor place a piece of gold wire in the places he has pierced,and when they heal which they will in a few days, you can remove the gold wire and the hole will remain there. You can then perform the above tests without the slightest danger or pain to yourself. This is a very sensational act, and commands a good salary.'

How to become a contortionist

'There are two styles of contortionist, the back bender and the front bender or leg worker. If you want to become a contortionist you must make up your mind to practise hard, just as when learning other acts. The old story that a contortionist rubs snake oil on himself is nonsense. You must make up your mind whether to be a front or back bender, as no one can do both at all well. Never have a full stomach when you practise or perform. All contortionists, including the very best, must loosen up or practise about twenty minutes before they introduce their performance; begin by rubbing your back with your hands and bend back as far as possible without straining yourself. Practise from five to twenty minutes every morning and evening, and in a short time you will be surprised at the results; in about twenty days you will be able to limber up and do all kinds of tricks. Don't miss one day's practice, as it will put you back more than a week; always work chest up, and draw your breath when bending back. To learn to be a contortionist you should not be over eighteen years of age, but a person of twenty-five or twenty-eight years can learn, but will find more difficulty in acquiring some of the tricks.'

Snake charming

'The prevailing idea that all snakes must have their teeth or fangs extracted before they can be handled is an erroneous one. All of the larger species, such as the pythons, boa constrictors and anacondas, are not poisonous, and their bite is no more harmful than that of a kitten, while if a cobra, a rattlesnake or a copperhead bites even himself he will surely die. A serpent's fangs cannot be extracted without bursting the poison bag, which would let the venom into their system and cause almost instant death. Where snakes are properly broken they can be handled by anyone possessing the necessary amount of courage. As a snake only attacks in self-defence, they are first taught that there is no intent to harm them. This is done by constant handling. If the snake is vicious at first a blanket is thrown over its head; the tamer takes it by the neck with one hand, grasping it by the middle with the other; in this position, holding it firmly but not too tightly, he slips a wire or elastic muzzle over the reptile's nose. A week's handling in this manner, as a rule, renders almost any serpent tractable. Poisonous serpents sometimes have their mouths sewn together with fine linen thread in such a manner that it cannot be seen at even close quarters. This may seem cruel, but it renders them safe.

'They shed their skin from three to four times a year, usually eating right after shedding. Their food consists of birds, rats, guinea-pigs and rabbits. The animal is given to them alive, when the serpent will pounce on it, crush it to death and swallow it whole. They should have a bath in lukewarm water and a little milk with two or three raw eggs stirred up in it, at least once a week. They will live sometimes a year or more on this diet alone. As all of the larger species come from tropical countries they must be kept very warm by means of woollen blankets and jugs or tanks of hot water.'

The secret of sword swallowing

'I can safely say that nine out of every ten persons imagine how erroneous this idea is; I have heard parties who ought to be well posted tell how the blade was in joints, and how each joint slipped into the other and finally into the handle. In Robert Houdini's *Memoirs* the author, in referring to an East Indian sword swallower's remarkable performances, advanced the idea that his throat was of a peculiar construction, different from the rest of mankind. There may be some truth in this, but I doubt it very much. Anyway, I eat and talk the same as other people, and I have never been able to discover any peculiar formation about my throat. I first saw this remarkable feat performed in the year 1874 by a Japanese, who told me there was no deception about it. I immediately made up my mind that I would be a sword swallower. In fact it had such an effect upon me that for months after I was trying to swallow knives, lead pencils, or anything I could lay my hands upon. However, I would not advise you to experiment with any of the above articles, but procure a finely polished, blunt-edged steel sword about twelve inches long, a half inch broad and a sixteenth of an inch in thickness, rub it on your coat sleeve, or with a piece of woollen cloth until it becomes blood-warm, then throw back your head (making a straight passage from mouth to stomach), and put it slowly down your throat. I find the greatest difficulty is in getting the head back far enough. Throw your head back as far as you can and look straight up at the ceiling. There is really no danger if properly done, yet a great deal of care should be taken, and if you aim at success remember the following rules: don't get excited but be calm, never attempt twice in succession, or in less than one hour after eating. Withdraw the blade immediately after swallowing. Keep it out of your windpipe. Practise and persevere, these are the most essential of all, and if lived up to success is certain.'

Dancing on broken glass with bare feet

'This novel and mysterious act is the latest sensation. If you want to be a regular glass dancer, to work in museums, circuses, side shows, etc., get yourself a box about four feet long, three feet wide and seven inches deep. Fill this box with small pieces of broken glass. The glass consists mostly of thick bottles, and it is a good idea to file the edges of the glass round if it is very sharp, but this is not really necessary. The glass *must* be broken in rather small pieces and be thick. The secret lies in this: the performer takes some resin that is smashed up fine as powder and rubs it on his feet. When he has resin on his feet he can go in the box of broken glass and jump around with bare feet and never need fear of cutting himself. It is best to practise a week or so before you attempt it before the public, so your feet will be used to the glass. If you only want to do the trick once a day you can break bottles before the eyes of the audience and dance on them, but in all cases it is best to have your own prepared glass. The resin used on your feet is common resin, and be sure to have plenty of it on your feet.'

INDEX

Printed by C. I. Thomas & Sons (Haverfordwest) Ltd.,
Press Buildings, Merlins Bridge, Haverfordwest, Pembrokeshire.